PARTNERSHIP IN RURAL EDUCATION

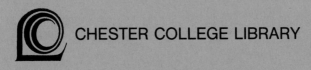

PARTNERSHIP IN RURAL EDUCATION

Church schools and teacher attitudes

Leslie J. Francis

Research Officer, Culham College Institute for Church Related Education

Collins

Collins Liturgical Publications
8 Grafton Street, London W1X 3LA

Distributed in Ireland by
Educational Company of Ireland
21 Talbot Street, Dublin 1

Collins Liturgical Australia
P.O. Box 3023, Sydney 2001

©1986 Leslie J. Francis
ISBN 0 00 599885 9
First published 1986

Data capture by Culham College Institute for Church Related Education
Phototypeset by Burgess & Son (Abingdon) Ltd
Printed by William Collins Sons & Co, Glasgow

CONTENTS

PREFACE

by the Bishop of London

The Church of England has recently been paying attention to the theme of partnership within the maintained system of education, the National Society's Discussion Paper 'A Future in Partnership', and the General Synod paper, 'Positive Partnership' (prepared for a General Synod debate in July 1985) being indicators of this interest. A book which sets out and analyses the results of research into 'Partnership in Rural Education' is therefore highly relevant to this current and doubtless continuing area of reflection and debate.

When discussions occur at central and national level it is important that they reveal an awareness of the local dimension. It can be very easy erroneously to assume that one has an adequate grasp of both the past and the present scene throughout the country. Hence the value of local studies.

In the first part of this book, Leslie Francis presents a valuable historical account of developments in one diocese. I am interested to note how one of the challenges to be found in the current educational debate in Church of England circles is shown to be no new phenomenon: what are we as a national Church to do with a system in which individual aided school governing bodies can make decisions regardless of their impact on diocesan policy and strategy and, indeed, in which individual dioceses can sometimes make irrevocable decisions which can affect the wider Church's contribution to and impact on the national scene?

It is often claimed that one of the factors that make a Church school distinctive is the particular commitment to be found among the teaching staff. Leslie Francis is therefore right to suggest that "to discover what is actually happening in church schools ... it is necessary to go to the teachers .... Ultimately it is the attitudes and practices of the teachers themselves which determine what the Church's partnership in rural education actually looks like in practice". Whether this study makes for comfortable, or uncomfortable reading, the attitudes revealed in it serve to underline the importance of diocesan education committees giving serious attention to the in-service training they provide for their church school teachers; this book certainly contains a considerable amount of material that could be used for stimulating many in-service training sessions.

I very much hope that this book will be used to help the governing bodies of church schools, in consultation with their staffs, parents, diocesan and parish representatives and other interested parties, to discuss, debate and reach consensus on the aims of their school. I also hope that more local studies will be forthcoming dealing with various aspects of the Church of England's participation in the country's education system so that our discussions and debates may be as informed as possible.

Graham Londin:
Chairman, General Synod Board of Education
November 1985

FOREWORD

This study of church schools had its origin in a working party set up by the St Edmundsbury and Ipswich diocesan education committee in 1981. The working party identified the need for a fresh research initiative into the contemporary character of church schools in a rural diocese. The opportunity to establish a research project in this area came from co-operation between the diocesan working party and the Culham College Institute for Church Related Education.

I am very grateful to the members of the church schools working party for their help and criticism in designing the study. Serving on this working party were Sally Fogden (member of the diocesan education committee), John Harvey (headmaster of St Peter and St Paul Church of England Aided Primary School, Eye), Gordon Highcock (assistant education officer, Suffolk County Council), Arthur Holifield (head-master of Debenham Church of England Controlled High School), Simon Pettitt (diocesan schools officer), Pat Scott (headmistress of Stonham Aspal Church of England Aided Primary School), Lawrence Trender (rector of Thornham Parva, Thornham Magna, Gislingham and Mellis) and Margaret Wickham (diocesan religious education adviser). I am particularly grateful to Margaret Wickham for the time and care she took in making personal contact with so many of the schools before inviting the teachers to co-operate in the project.

My thanks are also due to Haverhill Meat Products for printing the questionnaire; to the many teachers who completed the questionnaire; to the Department of Education and Science and to the local education authority for making available some statistical and historical data; to Iris Blake for giving me access to records in the National Society archives; to Tony Sparham for helping me find my way through diocesan records; to Boyd Wesley for working with me on the archives in the diocesan education office; to Sue Chapman, Geoffrey Duncan, John Gay, Helen Hughes, Kathleen Mills, Judith Muskett and Christine Wright for commenting on various drafts of the manuscript; to Carole Boorman, Clare Gowing and Kim Luckett for typing successive editions of the text; and to Alan Davies for phototypesetting.

Culham College Institute,   Leslie J. Francis
August 1985

9

1 INTRODUCTION

The historic link between church and school continues to be very noticeable, especially in rural areas. A number of Victorian school buildings stand adjacent to the church or to the old parsonage house, indicating the original ownership of the land on which they were built. Others proudly proclaim a biblical text over their main entrance or display the names of incumbent and churchwardens inscribed in the foundation stone. Their trust deeds continue to remind the school governors that their original intention included providing "moral and religious education according to the principles of the Church of England" and making special provision for the "children of the labouring, manufacturing and other poorer classes of the parish".

The link between church and school is by no means enshrined only in Victorian school architecture and nineteenth century trust deeds. Some of the most modern rural schools carry names like 'St James Church of England Voluntary Controlled' or 'All Saints Church of England Voluntary Aided'. Their foundation stones, laid in the 1970s, may well proclaim a text from *The New English Bible* and the name of the current bishop who presided at the official opening ceremony. The institutional link between these schools and the church is cemented through the role of the incumbent as a foundation governor, through the opportunity for denominational assemblies and, in some cases, through the provision of denominational religious instruction.

An important indication of the continued overall strength of the presence of the Church of England in primary education is given by the fact that in 1983 exactly one in four (25%) of the primary schools in England, including the middle schools deemed primary by the Department of Education and Science, were Church of England voluntary schools. However, although the Church of England is involved in the provision of a quarter of the primary school buildings, these Church of England schools provide places for considerably less than one quarter of the country's primary aged pupils. In 1983 one in six (17%) of the primary aged pupils within state maintained schools in England attended a Church of England voluntary school. Although there are many exceptions, the Church of England voluntary schools tend to be both smaller and more rural.

Although the proportion of church schools varies considerably, even from one rural diocese to another, it is highest in a number of rural areas. Indeed, in four local education authorities as many as half of the primary schools are Church of England voluntary schools, namely Oxfordshire (51%), Shropshire (50%), Somerset (50%) and Wiltshire (50%). In fourteen other rural local education authorities between one third and one half of the primary schools are Church of England voluntary schools, namely Dorset (47%), Worcestershire (45%), Lincolnshire (44%), Gloucestershire (42%), North Yorkshire (42%), Cumbria (40%), Suffolk (39%), Warwickshire (34%), Isle of Wight (34%), East Sussex (34%), Northamptonshire (33%); West Sussex (33%) and Leicestershire (33%).

The church school question

In the majority of cases, the rural Church of England school exists to serve the educational needs of a given community or set of communities. Although these are schools of a church related foundation, they are required to function as neighbourhood schools, just like the county schools in similar environments. This very fact presents an interesting set of theoretical and practical questions both for the churches themselves and for the educationalists concerned to promote an adequate concept of state maintained schools for an increasingly secular society. Today the church school system is undergoing increasing scrutiny and criticism not only from secular bodies but from within the churches themselves. To the objections raised by the British Humanist Association, the Socialist Education Association, the Runnymede Trust and the Swann Report must be added the voices of the Catholic Commission for Racial Justice, the group known as Christians Against Racism and Fascism, and the Church of England's Partners in Mission Consultation.

The British Humanist Association has been campaigning against the place of church schools within the state maintained system for a number of years. Their pamphlet, *Religion in Schools*, published in 1967, argues very strongly that the present dual system is an anachronism and accuses the church of abusing its privileged position by indoctrination. The British Humanist Association argues that the state should not be involved in sponsoring non-denominational Christian teaching in county schools and, still less, in financing and recognising the religious teaching of individual churches or religious bodies. They argue that religion should be left to the home and to the church, without either support or interference from the state.

The conclusions and recommendations of the British Humanist Association in their 1967 paper on the future of church schools are clear and unambiguous.

> Aided schools giving religious and moral education in accordance with the doctrines of a particular church or religious body should no longer continue as part of the system of schools maintained by rates and taxes. They should be taken over as county schools or left to the church to finance without state aid.
>
> Aided schools in 'single school areas' should be converted without delay into county schools. Their continued existence is wholly unjustifiable.
>
> Voluntary controlled schools should be ... converted into county schools.

Recently church schools have also come under close scrutiny by the Socialist Education Association in their discussion document, *The Dual System of Voluntary and County Schools*, published in 1981. This discussion document reflects a wide range of views within the Labour Party, from party members who find positive values in voluntary schools to those who oppose the segregation of education on religious lines. An appendix to this discussion document which marshals the case against church schools focuses on two primary objections.

The first objection concerns the problem of recognising religious privilege within a pluralist, multi-cultural, multi-faith society. This objection acknowledges that, if certain churches are allowed the privilege of operating voluntary schools within the state maintained system, the only fair consequence is to permit every sect and faith to have its own schools on the rates and taxes. It is argued that such a consequence would lead to "a disastrous running down of our secular education system. It would also lead to divisive sectarianism and some of the difficulties already evident in a place like Northern Ireland."

The second objection concerns the political problem of privilege itself within a socialist educational system. The discussion document summarises the problem like this.

> In simple terms, it is that the continuing existence of the segregated voluntary school sector will frustrate the achievement of the truly comprehensive system. It means that equal educational opportunity for all children will always be threatened, and that there can never be genuine parity between schools.

Another line of attack on church schools comes from the direction of racial discrimination. Ann Dummett and Julia McNeal's study, *Race and Church Schools*, sponsored by the Runnymede Trust and published in 1981, argues that the specifically Christian reference of church schools has a dual effect:

> Where there was a black Christian community, it had the effect of creating multiracial institutions; where the black community was not Christian, it had the effect of preventing this.

A similar criticism against church schools has come from some quarters within the churches themselves. The Catholic Commission for Racial Justice has said that some Catholic schools "pander to white parents' desire to send their children to a white school". A similar claim is made by the group Christians Against Racism and Fascism who state that "in some areas church schools have become white enclaves using religion as a means of discrimination".

The joint working party set up by the Catholic Commission for Racial Justice, the Department of Catholic Schools and the Laity Commission, in the report *Learning from Diversity*, published in 1984, takes the discussion of the problem of church schools in a multi-racial, multi-cultural society one stage further.

> Many Catholic schools have a pupil population which is predominantly white. As a result many Catholic children have an educational experience which is, in this respect, narrow. They do not have the opportunity to mix with black children nor do they have the opportunity to mix with children of other Christian denominations or of other faiths. Moreover the predominantly white Catholic school in a racially mixed area can be seen as a 'white island' and a divisive anomaly in an area which faces the difficult task of struggling to become a cohesive multiracial and multicultural community.

On the Anglican front, the discussion paper produced by the General Synod of the Church of England Board of Education in 1984, *Schools and Multi-Cultural Education*, also acknowledges the potential divisiveness of church schools in a multi-cultural context. At the same time the Anglican report emphasises that church schools can also function as important centres of reconciliation among peoples of different races and creeds.

The church school question is a central issue focused by the Swann Report, *Education for All*, published in 1985, as the findings of the committee of inquiry into the education of children from ethnic minority groups. After reviewing the arguments for and against separate voluntary schools for other ethnic and religious groups, the majority voice of the committee stresses "misgivings about the implications and consequences of 'separate' provision of any kind".

Having come to this view, the majority voice of the committee faces the consequence that:

> our conclusions about the desirability of denominational voluntary aided schools for Muslims or other groups, by extension seriously call into question the long established dual system of educational provision in this country and particularly the role of the churches in the provision of education .... We believe therefore that the time has come for the DES, in consultation with religious and educational bodies, to consider the relevant provisions of the 1944 Act to see whether or not alterations are required in a society that is now radically different.

No less than six members of the committee of inquiry dissented from this conclusion and formulated a completely different minority recommendation, not only supporting the provisions of the 1944 Education Act concerning voluntary schools, but clearly wishing to see other ethnic and religious groups enabled to benefit from these provisions. The minority voice stresses:

> We believe that it is unjust at the present time not to recommend that positive assistance should be given to ethnic minority communities who wish to establish voluntary aided schools in accordance with the 1944 Education Act.

In an oral statement to the House of Commons on the afternoon of 14 March 1985, following the publication of the Swann Committee Report, Sir Keith Joseph, Secretary of State for Education, made an immediate response to the voluntary aided school question.

> But to forestall unfounded fears or hopes the Government wishes to make clear that it cannot accept four recommendations in the report. We do not intend to change the present statutory requirements for daily collective worship and for religious education in maintained schools. Nor do we wish in any way to call in question the present dual system of county and voluntary school ....

The clear division of opinion within the committee of inquiry, together with the Education Secretary's immediate response, adds a new sharpness and immediacy to the debate about the future of church schools within a multi-cultural society.

The report of the Church of England's Partners in Mission Consultation, *To a Rebellious House*, published in 1981, attacks church schools from a completely different basis. This report argues that the church has put too much of its energy and resources into church schools during the past hundred years without achieving sufficient benefit in term of the church's work of mission and nurture. The report recommends that the churches should attempt to release some of their assets currently tied up in church schools and redirect these assets in other educational areas.

The small school question

The real threat to the church school system, as it has historically evolved, comes less from the explicit challenging of its educational philosophy than from the gradual erosion of its actual provision of school sites. As a matter of fact, church schools have tended to be the smaller schools: from the time of the 1944 Education Act onwards there has been a growing policy to close small schools and to transfer their pupils to larger schools in neighbouring communities.

Because the process of small school closure has been conducted by local education authorities in a piecemeal and *ad hoc* fashion, until recently little attention has been given to the cumulative implications of such a policy on the Church of England's stake in the provision of the national system of state maintained schools. The Department of Education and Science figures for primary school provision in England and Wales in 1953 indicate that 35.3% of primary schools belonged to the Church of England or the Church of Wales. By 1963 the proportion had fallen to 31.1%, while by 1973 the proportion had fallen further to 25.6%. In other words, during a twenty year period, the number of Church of England and Church of Wales primary schools in England and Wales had been reduced from 8,251 to 5,860.

This sharp fall in the number of church schools during the 1950s and 1960s can be largely accounted for in terms of the closure of small schools. Although during this twenty year period the proportion of state maintained primary schools owned by the Church of England fell by 10%, the proportion of school places provided within Church of England schools fell by less than 5%. In 1953 Church of England schools provided 21% of the state maintained primary school places; by 1973 this proportion had fallen to 16.4%.

The next ten year period between 1973 and 1983 saw comparatively little further reduction in the church school position. During this period 721 Church of England or Church of Wales schools were closed, reducing their share from 25.6% to 24.3% of the total primary provision.

The small school question is itself a complex area of debate. The Plowden Report, *Children in their Primary Schools*, published in 1967, reflected the thinking of the 1960s, when many small schools were being closed, in its section on education in rural areas. Here the report recommends that schools with an age range of 5-11 should have at least three classes, each covering two age groups. The case against small schools was being argued not only in economic terms, but in educational terms as well.

The educational argument against small schools suggests that small schools can restrict their pupils' social, emotional and intellectual development. Small schools, it is argued, limit the pupils' social opportunities to mix with their peers, deprive them of the benefit of working with the range of teachers needed to offer different skills, and restrict their acquaintance with educational resources, curriculum materials and extra-curricular activities.

The 1970s, however, saw a change of emphasis on the small school question. A number of specialist research projects, like the Rural Education Research Unit in the Department of Education at Bangor, the Study of the Social Effects of Rural Primary Schools Re-organisation based in the University of Aston and the Project on Rural Community and the Small School at the University of Aberdeen, all began to question the truth of the educational claims made against the small school. Counter arguments also began to emerge concentrating on the implications of the link between home and school, the detrimental effects of bussing and of long days away from home on young children, and the wider social consequences of community disintegration stemming from the closure of community schools.

In 1978 the National Association for the Support of Small Schools was formed. In 1979 the Advisory Centre for Education produced a booklet, *Schools under Threat*, giving guidelines on how to fight a school closure. By 1981 the Cambridge Policy Group had produced *A Positive Approach to Rural Primary Schools*. At the same time, lessons were being taken from the Organisation for Economic Co-operation and Development's Education in Sparsely Populated Areas Project, from the re-opening of small schools in Norway and Finland and from the reversal of the policy to close small schools in New Zealand.

The 1980s, however, are seeing yet another mood. Now local education authorities are increasingly hard-pressed by central government to make all the financial savings that they can. The small school debate has now been firmly moved from the educational and social arenas into the financial arena. Unit costs, it is argued, are higher in small schools. Financial savings can be secured by closing small schools and concentrating pupils in larger classes in bigger schools, even after allowing for the cost of extra transport.

The white paper *Better Schools* presented to parliament by the Secretary of State for Education and Science and the Secretary of State for Wales in March 1985 presents some clear policy statements about the minimum size of schools. It is the duty of local education authorities, it states, to ensure that schools are large enough to justify sufficient teachers to satisfy the white paper's recommendations for the curriculum. In 1981 the Department of Education and Science's circular 'Falling Rolls and Surplus Places' advises a minimum primary school size of 100 pupils. The 1985 recommendation is that "it is desirable that 5-11 schools should have at least one form of entry. Because of the smaller number of year groups 7-11 schools need at least two forms of entry." The white paper recognises that "such factors as geography, population sparsity, and the need for denominational choice ... may sometimes necessitate unusually small schools". However, the white paper also issues the clear warning that such small schools can only be maintained at the expense of the larger schools from which they divert resources. Looking particularly closely at the small school question, the white paper recommends:

> the number of pupils in a primary school should not in general fall below the level at which a complement of three teachers is justified, since it is inherently difficult for a very small school to be educationally satisfactory. But geographical and social factors need to be given their full weight. In isolated communities it is often right, given appropriate augmentation of resources, to retain a small village school.

It seems sensible, therefore, to try to predict what the implications of another round of small school closures might look like for the Church of England's stake in the state maintained sector of primary schools. Such predictions are uncertain, especially since smallness is such a slippery concept. A useful guideline which has been discussed for a number of years is the minimum size of 60 pupils. Sixty pupils is the minimum mentioned by the Gittins report in 1967 and recommended, for example, in the Wiltshire County Council Education Committee policy statement, *Small Rural Schools in Wiltshire*, issued in 1969. The Gloucestershire County Council Education Committee was asked to consider the same figure towards the end of 1984. Certainly a school with fewer than 60 pupils is unlikely to feel confident about retaining the minimum of three teachers recommended by the white paper *Better Schools*.

If all small schools in England with less than 60 pupils were closed this would again radically redraw the map of the Church of England's provision in primary education. Using the Department of Education and Science's figures for January 1983 as a guideline, 60% of all schools closed on this criterion would be Church of England schools. If such a

17

policy were to be implemented, the Church of England's stake in the total primary provision in England would be further reduced from 25% to 20% of schools.

The majority of such closures would, understandably, occur in the English counties rather than in the metropolitan districts. It is, therefore, instructive to calculate separately the implications of such a policy for the English counties independently of the metropolitan districts. In 1983 Church of England provision accounted for 31% of the primary schools in the English counties. If all schools under 60 pupils were to be closed, the Church of England's stake in the English counties would be reduced to 24% of primary schools.

The precise implications of such a policy vary greatly from one local education authority to another. For example, in Oxfordshire the Church of England's stake would be reduced from 51.4% to 42.8%; in Herefordshire and Worcestershire from 44.9% to 35.7%; in Gloucestershire from 42.8% to 34%; in Cumbria from 39.7% to 26.5%; in Suffolk from 38.5% to 25.3% and in Norfolk from 34.2% to 25.5%. In Lancashire the reduction would be 33.8% to 30.1%.

Faced with the probability of such an imminent and radical reduction in its stake in rural primary education, the time is right for the Church of England to re-assess why it wants to be involved in the state maintained sector of schools, what it hopes to give through such involvement and what it hopes to gain from it.

The question of partnership

The policy statements of the Church of England itself have not been slow to acknowledge and to wrestle with the problems and opportunities of the church's continued close involvement in the state maintained sector of education. The early 1970s saw the publication and debate of two key reports: the Durham Report, *The Fourth R* and the Carlisle Report, *Partners in Education*. Through these reports the Church of England evolved a contemporary theory to account for its continued presence in the state maintained sector of education based on two fundamental principles. The first principle speaks in terms of a *partnership* between church and state to share the responsibility for the education of the nation's children. The second principle draws a distinction between what the church understands to be its two contributions to this partnership, a *general* concern and a *domestic* concern.

The church's general concern in education evolves from a theology of service which argues that the church has a responsibility to make its presence felt in education but without seeking to use this presence as a platform for evangelism or proselytism. The church's domestic concern has come to be associated with a theology of nurture which argues that the church has a responsibility to induct the children of its members into the heritage of the believing community. The delicate balancing trick which this theory involves concerns the satisfaction of both the general and the domestic functions without on the one hand alienating those churchmen committed to distinctive church education and on the other hand alarming the secular educationalists who accuse the church of confusing education with indoctrination.

The recent Green Paper for discussion published in 1984 by The National Society (Church of England) for Promoting Religious Education carries the title *A Future in Partnership*. This title builds on what is now the well-established notion of the partnership between church and state in the education of the nation's children, growing out of the 1944 Education Act, and then proceeds to reinterpret the concept of partnership within a new context. The emphasis of this paper is on arguing the advantages for a balance of power in state maintained education over an increasing trend towards educational dominance by central government, a trend characterised by the author of the discussion paper as 'centrism'.

In *A Future in Partnership* the church is seen as one component in an educational partnership which offsets the claims of central government in determining educational policy and practice. In this sense the churches' contribution is evaluated alongside that of other political, community, parental and professional interests, as apparently represented through parents, governors, and so on. It is argued that the maintenance of church schools gives the church an institutional credibility in this context. In 1984 the Church of England is testing out the possibility of seeing the weight of its rationale for involvement in education to be in terms of balance, partnership and voluntarism, rather than in terms of denominationalism, religious distinctiveness or the potential divisiveness implied in the old concept of 'the dual system'.

The development of this essentially secular rationale for the churches' continued involvement in state maintained education raises the two key questions as to why the church should want to suppress its distinctive gospel in the course of social service and why the secular state should want to accept a secular service motivated by a religious tradition. In the last analysis, the argument is unlikely to convince either the committed church-goers who desire a distinctively Christian education for their children or the committed secularists who argue that there is no place left for religious involvement in a secular educational system.

The research question

While policy statements provide one set of insights into the contemporary concept of the church school, both diocesan education committees and local education authorities might be forgiven for wondering to what extent the policy voiced in current discussion papers is in fact reflected in the practice of the local church schools within their own areas. Perhaps of even more immediate significance is the question inevitably raised in the minds of the parents who send their children to a church school, whether by choice or necessity. What are the reasonable expectations which they can have of their neighbourhood Church of England school? Are these expectations in any sense different from those appropriate within comparable county schools? After all, many parents would argue that it is merely on account of the accidents of history and geography that they find themselves within the catchment area of a church or a county school. My aim in this book, therefore, is to turn attention away from what the church is *saying* about its church schools at a policy level and attempt to uncover what in fact the church is currently *doing* through its church schools.

In order to discover what is actually happening in church schools, I believe that it is necessary to go to the teachers who are working in the church school system. While the national church, the diocese, the local church and the school governors, alongside the Department of Education and Science and the local education authority, can all have a part in defining and describing what they think can or should take place in church schools, the quality and character of the education provided in these schools rests very much in the hands of the headteachers and the class teachers who work with them. Ultimately it is the attitudes and practices of the teachers themselves which determine what the churches' partnership in rural education actually looks like in practice.

Any attempt to make a careful and detailed study of the attitudes and perceptions of teachers is bound to be a time-consuming and slow process. My way of making such a task manageable has been by restricting my interest specifically to the question of church primary schools in a rural diocese – in fact to scrutinise the church school system where it is strongest. When the resources to undertake research are limited, I believe that it is more profitable to concentrate on one limited geographical area in depth than to attempt a national study at a superficial level. What I have been able to do is to uncover the facts for one diocese, the diocese of St Edmundsbury and Ipswich, and to do so with the full support, co-operation and encouragement of the diocesan education committee. It remains for other researchers, following my lead, to test the extent to which it is sensible to generalise from this diocese to other areas in the Church of England.

Before discussing the way in which the survey of teachers' attitudes was set up in the diocese of St Edmundsbury and Ipswich, I attempt in chapter two to put the church school debate in its historic context. I begin by tracing in brief outline the development of denominational interest in education from the founding of the National Society in 1811, through the 1870 and 1944 Education Acts, to the present day. Then I turn in much greater detail to an examination of the fluctuating fortunes of the church school system in the diocese of St Edmundsbury and Ipswich itself, from the foundation of the diocese in 1914, through the restructuring of the 1944 Education Act, the development of a three-tier system of schools as a response to secondary reorganisation in the late 1960s and the trauma of local government reorganisation in the 1970s, to the present day. During this period, the proportion of schools in the diocese which are church related falls from 68% of all schools to 39% of primary schools and 9% of secondary schools. The absence of a strong diocesan policy on church schools has largely left each church school to determine its own identity and to fight for its own survival. This story is not untypical of other dioceses in the Church of England.

Against this historical background, chapter three moves on to the main section of this book and discusses the design of the survey into the perceptions and attitudes of those who actually teach in the church schools in the diocese. This chapter examines the way in which the research grew from and was sponsored by a working party commissioned by the the diocesan education committee itself. It also discusses the design and preliminary testing of the research questionnaire, the sampling strategy, including the way in which the questionnaire was distributed, and the kind of response it received. In other words, this chapter provides the technical background against which the results of the survey might be assessed.

The results of the survey are then presented in chapters four through nine. Chapter four begins the story by saying something about the teachers themselves. After looking at the age structure and sex ratio, this chapter turns the focus to the religious affiliation, church attendance and community involvement of those who teach in church schools. Have those who find themselves teaching in church schools generally set out to select for themselves a post in a denominational voluntary school, or is it mainly a matter of chance that they find themselves in a church school? The statistics of this chapter show that just one in three of the teachers in Church of England schools actually express a preference for working in a church school, while some would specifically prefer not to be teaching in a church school at all.

Chapter five singles out for attention the teachers' attitudes to the church school system. It does so by identifying nine key issues concerned with the character of church schools. These are the teachers' attitudes towards (1) the staffing requirements of church schools, (2) the admissions policy operated by church schools, (3) the direction in which church schools should move in the future, (4) the criticisms voiced against the church school system, (5) the tension between commitment and neutrality in education, (6) the place and character of religious education in the church school, (7) the relationship between church schools and the diocese, (8) the contact between the school and the local church and (9) the involvement of the clergy in the life of the church school. Although the majority of those teaching in church schools have not necessarily sought out a place for themselves in the church school system, the data demonstrate that the majority of them hold fairly positive attitudes to the system and only a very small proportion would wish to see the church withdraw from state maintained education.

Chapter six moves from the teachers' attitudes to the church school to look in detail at their more general perceptions of what is required of them as teachers in the classroom. What sort of education can parents expect their children to receive if they attend a Church of England voluntary primary school? In order to provide a thorough description of the teachers' perceptions of what they are doing and hoping to achieve in the classroom, this chapter identifies eight key areas. It examines the teachers' understanding of (1) the curriculum in general, (2) religious education in particular, (3) the notion of the school as a Christian community, (4) the kind of ethos to be communicated by the school, (5) the relationship between the school and the local community, (6) the contribution of the school to the moral development of the pupils, (7) the theory and practice of traditional educational methods and (8) the theory and practice of progressive educational methods. The picture which emerges from this analysis is one of basically conscientious teachers who, while tending to favour traditional educational methods, nevertheless succeed in integrating many of the more progressive educational ideas within the framework of a comparatively traditional philosophy.

While chapter six examines the educational characteristics of the rural church school, it is not able to say to what extent the teachers regard these characteristics as a direct or even an indirect consequence of the schools' religious foundation. Chapter seven, therefore, takes the story one stage further to explore the teachers' perceptions of the distinctiveness of the church school. It achieves this goal by retracing the eight areas already discussed in the previous chapter, but from a different perspective. This time, instead of asking the teachers to rate the importance which should be given to a range of educational goals, we ask them to assess how much attention they reckon Church of England schools should give to these goals compared with county schools. The data presented in this chapter indicate that teachers in church schools do have clear and distinctive notions regarding the ways in which these church schools can and cannot differ from county schools. In short, they continue to practise the belief that church schools can and should be religiously different from county schools. For them notions of partnership do not completely elide notions of denominationalism.

While chapters five, six and seven present a detailed overview of attitudes towards the church school system, the characteristics of church schools and the distinctiveness of church schools, chapter eight recognises that this overview tends to disguise the large range of opinions among the teachers themselves. In order to correct the balance, chapter eight reanalyses the data with a range of more sophisticated statistical techniques in order to develop mathematical models which begin to account for the differences in the attitudes held by various groups of teachers.

Chapter nine recognises that, beneath all the statistical generalisations of the previous chapters, there are a number of distinctive individuals, the men and women who teach in church schools. The questionnaire used in this study enables us to make statistical generalisations, but it also preserves the uniqueness of each individual. In the last analysis, one of the greatest benefits of sociological generalisations is the way in which these generalisations help us to gain insight into the individuals whom we know and among whom we work. With this in mind, chapter nine presents detailed profiles of just seven of the teachers who co-operated in the study. Needless to say, in writing these profiles the teachers' anonymity has been totally preserved. The names attributed both to the schools and to the teachers in this chapter are fictitious, although the descriptions are based totally on fact.

The opportunity to meet a few of the teachers close up brings into sharper perspective the wide range of views held in the staff rooms of rural church primary schools and the important implications of these views for those concerned with the future of the church school system. When all is said and done, it is precisely the views and attitudes of the individual teachers in the specific schools which determine the way in which the church school system is interpreted and implemented in any given situation.

Finally, chapter ten turns the focus of this book away from the research data, back to those responsible for criticising and developing the churches' continued involvement in the state maintained sector of education. It does this by posing a set of key questions, arising from the earlier chapters which discuss in detail the views of those who teach in church schools. While research of this nature can never lead directly to an unambiguous set of recommendations for policy, such research does provide the essential data against which policy needs to be formulated if such policy statements are indeed to speak sensibly to the contemporary situation and not to be left merely in a theoretical vacuum.

If there is to be a 'future in partnership', then this future needs both to understand the historical trends of the past, from which it has developed, and to gauge sensitively the contemporary reality of the present, in which it will be nurtured. If the present research project helps the churches in this way, many of the hopes of the diocesan working party which first initiated it will have been realised.

2 HISTORICAL PERSPECTIVE

In 1984 the statistics provided by the Department of Education and Science indicated that there were a total of 363 state maintained schools in the county of Suffolk. Of these 363 schools, 116 (32%) were voluntary schools operated in association with the Church of England and 14 (3.9%) were voluntary schools operated in association with the Roman Catholic Church. The same source of statistical information indicated that these schools provided places for 93,588 full-time pupils. This calculation follows the convention of counting two part-time pupils as one full-time pupil. Of these 93,588 pupils, 12,594 (13.5%) were located in Church of England schools and 2,956 (3.2%) were located in Roman Catholic schools.

A somewhat different picture emerges if we decide to review separately the statistics for primary and secondary schools. Although much of the county of Suffolk has been reorganised on a three tier system of education, the Department of Education and Science statistics still enable the traditional dichotomy between primary and secondary to be calculated by the process of 'deeming' some middle schools as primary and others as secondary.

Looked at from this perspective, there were, at January 1984, 283 state maintained primary schools in the county of Suffolk, catering for 39,452 pupils. The Church of England stake in the state maintained sector of primary education accounts for 109 (38.5%) of the primary schools and for 8,873 (22.5%) of the primary pupils. The Roman Catholic stake accounts for 11 (3.9%) of the primary schools and 1,555 (3.9%) of the primary pupils.

Also at January 1984, there were 80 state maintained secondary schools (including middle deemed secondary) in the county of Suffolk, catering for 54,136 pupils. The Church of England stake in the state maintained sector of secondary education accounts for 7 (8.8%) of the secondary schools and for 3,722 (6.9%) of the secondary pupils. The Roman Catholic stake accounts for 3 (3.8%) of the secondary schools and for 1,401 (2.6%) of the secondary pupils.

These statistics highlight two important facts about the provision of Church of England schools in the diocese. First, the involvement of the Church of England is much higher in the primary sector of education than in the secondary. Second, at the primary level, the Church of England's involvement accounts for a much higher proportion of the school buildings than of the pupils. This is because the Church of England primary schools tend to be the smaller schools in the county.

In order to understand how this situation has arisen, it is necessary to delve briefly into the national story of the church's involvement in education in England, and then to look in some detail at how the national issues influence the development in Suffolk.

NATIONAL STORY

Although our view in the 1980s clearly attributes to the state the central responsibility for providing a national system of education, it needs to be remembered that the state has only accepted that responsibility comparatively recently. The initiative during the eighteenth and nineteenth centuries in the provision of education for the nation's children came not from the state, but from the churches.

The churches' early initiative in education is seen in a variety of ways. In 1698 the Society for Promoting Christian Knowledge began its work of encouraging the establishment of charity schools. In 1780 Robert Raikes started Sunday schools which were intended to provide education both in religion and secular subjects. In 1808 a group of Free Churchmen founded the Royal Lancastrian Society from which the British and Foreign Schools Society emerged in 1814. In 1811 a group of Anglicans founded the National Society 'for the education of the children of the poor in the principles of the established church'.

When the state first entered the field of public education in 1833, it did so not by establishing state schools, but by distributing public funds to the National Society and the British and Foreign Schools Society. They received a grant of £20,000 to help with school buildings. Other church groups saw these public funds becoming available for the promotion of church-related schools and established administrative machinery in order to claim their share of the state's beneficence. In 1843 the Methodist conference decided to enter the field of providing voluntary day schools and received its first state grant in 1847. Also in 1847 the Roman Catholic Church established the Catholic Poor School Committee, which, after some delay, was recognised as an authority able to receive grants from the state. Between 1833 and 1870 the state's only contribution to public education was through grants to these voluntary societies. By 1870 the principle that public schools were in the hands of the churches was well established.

1870 Education Act

The problem with voluntary initiative was that the provision was erratic over the whole country. The Elementary Education Act of 1870 did two things in response to this erratic provision. First, it permitted the schools founded by the voluntary societies to continue and gave them official entitlement to grants-in-aid. Second, local school boards were established to build their own schools in areas where voluntary school provision was inadequate. Board schools were intended to make good the gaps of the voluntary school system and not to replace that system. At the same time, the possibility of the establishment of board schools served to spur on the voluntary bodies to maintain and to increase their share in the national provision of schools. Thus, according to the 1870 Education Act, the churches found themselves holding a form of partnership with the state in the educational system of England.

While the Church of England shared its role in the provision of schools during the nineteenth century with the Roman Catholic Church and with many of the Free Churches, the precise nature of the Church of England's role in this area remained quite distinctive. As the established church of the realm, the Church of England conceived its role in much broader terms than the other churches. Church of England schools were often established with the explicit intention of providing education for the nation's children, not as an alternative educational system for the children of church members.

The next national landmark after the 1870 Education Act was the 1902 Education Act which established what has come to be known as 'the dual system'. Educational administration was transferred from the old school boards to the new local education authorities. The new local education authorities were also given control over the secular education in voluntary schools. Board schools were named 'provided' schools; voluntary schools were named 'non-provided' schools. The most significant feature of this Act is that both provided and non-provided schools were to receive rate aid.

Between 1902 and 1944 the dual system continued in spite of the churches' increasing financial difficulty in maintaining their commitment to schools, and in spite of the Fisher Education Bill's abortive attempt to introduce a unitary system in 1921. In fact, by the time of the 1936 Education Act the partnership between the church and state had

27

become so much part of the English educational system that the local education authorities were empowered to enter further into agreements with the churches to assist financially towards the erection of church senior schools.

1944 Education Act

The system of church schools which we know today is a direct result of the reconstitution of the educational system of England after the Second World War as embodied in the 1944 Education Act. At the heart of its thinking the 1944 Education Act envisaged the provision of secondary education for all. To make this possible, a large number of schools required extension, modernisation and re-equipment. On the one hand, the churches could not afford to maintain the voluntary schools and to bring them up to the new standards required. On the other hand, the state could not afford to buy up the church schools and was reluctant to annexe them. In short, the denominational schools presented a major political problem.

In the debate surrounding the formulation of the 1944 Education Act, the churches were themselves divided on their understanding of the future of the voluntary schools. The main body of Free Church opinion advocated the replacement of the dual system by a unified state system. They argued that the Christian presence in education could best be preserved through the agreed syllabus teaching of religious education in state schools. Some Anglicans also took this line. Other Anglicans wished to retain church voluntary schools. After prolonged negotiations, a compromise solution between the churches and the state continued the dual system and even strengthened it. As a consequence of the 1944 Education Act, voluntary schools were individually given the choice of two different statuses, 'aided' and 'controlled'. This choice was designed to enable those schools which could afford to retain a high level of independence to be able to do so, while those that either could not afford or did not desire to retain such a high level of independence, could nevertheless retain something of their church-related character.

The voluntary aided school approximated the status of the non-provided school, and involved the churches in continued financial liability. The churches were responsible for external repairs to the school building, necessary improvements and extensions to existing school buildings, and the provision of new school buildings. Government grant aid was made available to meet a percentage of this cost. Initially this contribution was determined as 50%. Subsequently, the proportion has been raised by steps to 85%. The local education authority is responsible for all other running costs of the aided school. In return for their continued financial involvement, the churches retained the right to appoint two-thirds of the school managers and to provide denominational religious instruction and denominational worship.

The voluntary controlled school gave the churches reduced rights, but involved no on-going financial liability. In this case, the churches retained the right to appoint one-third of the school managers. Religious instruction is to be given according to the agreed syllabus of the local education authority, but parents may ask for some denominational teaching "during not more than two periods in each week". Providing the teaching staff of the controlled school exceeds two, up to one fifth of the staff can be "selected for their fitness and competence to give such religious instruction". These are called 'reserved teachers'. The daily act of worship can also be denominational. The local education authority is entirely responsible for financing the voluntary controlled school.

A third category of voluntary school provided for in the 1944 Education Act is the 'special agreement' school. This category continued to honour the arrangements negotiated between local education authorities and the churches as a result of the 1936 Education Act, the implementation of which had been interrupted by the war. For most practical purposes the provisions regarding religious instruction, worship, finance and school management are basically the same as for voluntary aided status, except in relationship to the appointment of staff.

The choice between voluntary aided and voluntary controlled status was the responsibility of the governors or managers of each church school. They needed to weigh up the advantages of voluntary aided status against the cost and their ability to meet that cost. While each church school is an autonomous body, the diocese is in the position to offer advice, guidance and, of course, financial aid if it should both wish and be able to afford to do so. In the absence of an agreed central policy for the whole of the Church of England on the comparable merits of aided and controlled status, each diocese formulated its own recommendations which the schools within its area could choose to follow or to ignore, at least as far as their independent sources of finance would permit. Some dioceses, like London, Southwark and Blackburn, opted heavily for aided status, while others, like Bristol, York, Coventry and Lichfield, opted mainly for controlled status.

LOCAL STORY

The national story has been a comparatively easy tale to tell because a number of historians had already well prepared the ground. The telling of the local story is a much more difficult task; because others had not already prepared the ground before me, I needed to rely entirely on primary sources. The four areas in which I looked for these primary sources were the diocese, the headquarters of the National Society, the local education authority and the Department of Education and Science. None of these four areas was straightforward.

The local education authority now covering the county of Suffolk was formed in 1974, at the time of local government reorganisation, from an amalgamation of the three local education authorities formerly responsible for Suffolk East, Suffolk West and the borough of Ipswich. Local government reorganisation had apparently been a good opportunity for radically pruning the educational archives. While the Department of Education and Science is able to provide aggregated national figures for denominational schooling for each year from 1947 to the present day, it was able to provide separate figures according to denominational classification for the county of Suffolk only from 1967 onwards.

While the National Society keeps a file on all schools with which it has had some formal contact, these records are referenced on the basis of neither county nor diocese. The National Society archives provided an invaluable resource for checking on schools already identified by some other means, but not for initially identifying the appropriate schools. The main source of information upon which the local story can be told rests with the diocesan records.

The diocese of St Edmundsbury and Ipswich was formed in 1914 from part of the diocese of Norwich. The diocesan education committee has, fortunately, kept a complete set of minutes from its inaugural meeting until the present day. Although by no means all the decisions regarding the future of individual church schools in the diocese have been recorded in the minutes of the diocesan education committee, these accounts have provided the main clues to the local story. Less happily, a number of the files on individual schools and relating to specific policy issues had been stored for far too long in a damp cellar to be of much value.

When the new diocese was formed in 1914, there was the possibility that it would be coterminous with the county boundaries of Suffolk itself. One deanery in the north-east of the county, around Lowestoft, strongly resisted the notion of being severed from the diocese of Norwich. The new diocese, therefore, was not made coterminous with the county boundaries. This compounds the difficulties involved in drawing together information provided by the diocese, the local education authority and the Department of Education and Science.

Summary trends

I decided to take the formation of the diocese in 1914 as the starting point for my attempt to unravel the local story of the history of church schools in the area. In 1915 the diocese of St Edmundsbury and Ipswich published its first year book, listing the names of the 521 parishes thought to be in the diocese. According to this year book, these 521 parishes supported a total of 404 rate aided elementary schools. 275 (68%) of these schools are classified in the year book as church schools and 129 (32%) are classified as provided schools. During the next few years subsequent editions of the year book rectified a few misclassifications. Almost an equal number of misclassifications were corrected in both directions, leaving the basic ratio between church schools and provided schools unaffected.

As a first indication of the trend in the provision of church schools in the diocese from the formation of the diocese to the present day, I set out to trace what had happened to the church schools operating in the diocese in 1915. At the time of writing I have been successful in tracing the history of all but three of these schools. It seems likely that there were in fact 273 church schools operative in the diocese in 1915. The general picture is, then, one of steady closure, at the average rate of two or three a year through until the mid-1970s.

During the first five years of the life of the diocese, just three church schools were closed. During the 1920s, 31 church schools were closed or transferred to the local education authority. During the 1930s, 27 church schools were closed or transferred. A further 26 church schools were closed or transferred during the 1940s, and another 20 during the 1950s. During the 1960s, the toll rises to 38 church schools, and a further 20 are added to the list during the 1970s. This means that of the 273 church schools thought to have been operating in the diocese in 1915, 105 survived into the 1980s, 18 of them with aided status and 87 with controlled status. A full picture of this situation is given in tables 2.1 through 2.3.

Alongside this situation of the steady closure of 168 church schools in the diocese during the past 70 years, 8 new schools have been brought into the church schools system. A new school was established in Bury St Edmunds in 1937. As a result of the 1944 Education Act, the endowed Grammar school in Bury St Edmunds was enlisted as a church controlled school, with the greatest of reluctance on the part of its governors. A new secondary school, originally conceived in 1936, was eventually opened in Debenham in 1964. Finally, the introduction of the three tier system of schools to parts of the county of Suffolk saw the establishment of five church middle schools during the early 1970s. An aided middle school was established in Bury St Edmunds, while controlled middle schools were established in Butley, Newmarket, Stanton and Sudbury.

While the counting of school buildings is a useful index in assessing the changes that have taken place in the Anglican church's involvement in the provision of statutory education in the diocese, it is at best only a partial index. The statistics which would help to complete the picture concern the actual number of pupils in church schools and in county schools throughout the diocese. The facts that the Department of Education and Science have not published and have not systematically kept central records of the denominational breakdown for separate local education authorities and that many local records were lost at the time of local government reorganisation mean that these statistics are not available much before 1970. I am grateful to the local education authority and to the Department of Education and Science for making available to me such information as they possess, and this is summarised in table 2.4. The point made by this table is that in 1967 the Church of England schools accounted for 17.6% of the total school population in state maintained education within the county. By 1982 this proportion had fallen to 13.5%.

1944 Education Act

The gradual erosion of the church's stake in the provision of schools from the time of the formation of the diocese until the eve of the 1944 Education Act goes almost unnoticed in the minute books of the diocesan education committee. There was a stirring in 1925 when Her Majesty's Inspectorate placed in class A of the blacklist 5 church schools in East Suffolk and 4 in West Suffolk, while 10 church schools in East Suffolk and 20 in West Suffolk were placed in class B. The minutes record that this means that "nine schools were condemned as unsuitable and 30 as requiring considerable expenditure on them, and a remark was made that it was not to be supposed that this included all the schools upon which managers might be called upon to make alterations and improvements". The policy committee of the diocesan board of education lamented the lack of diocesan funds and formulated the recommendation "that at present all church schools should be kept if possible, but managers are not to be encouraged to rebuild or embark on expensive alterations". The individual schools were left to seek their own salvation.

After the Second World War, the debate surrounding the 1944 Education Act brought the question concerning the future of church schools very much more clearly into focus. The burning issue of the moment was whether to encourage the managers of church schools to struggle with the financial implications of claiming aided status or to accept the alternative of controlled status. Opinion in the diocese was divided on the merits of aided status. The consensus of the diocesan education committee, perhaps led by the suffragan Bishop of Dunwich, seemed to favour working for aided status. The July 1944 meeting of the diocesan education committee carried unanimously a resolution proposed by the Bishop of Dunwich strongly advocating that as many schools as possible should be retained as aided schools and that a separate appeal for church schools should be discussed in the diocese.

The diocesan bishop, however, took a strong line in the opposite direction. He argued that the financial priority of the diocese should be raising the stipends of the clergy, and that the limited resources available for education would be better deployed in the church's training colleges. The diocesan bishop in question is Richard Brook, who had been appointed in 1941. As a former headmaster of a public school, he seems to have had firm views on education.

Richard Brook's method of dealing with educational issues became apparent at a special meeting of the diocesan board of education in 1943. This meeting re-affirmed the responsibility of the church to provide education in the doctrine and worship of the Christian faith for those children with whom it was connected, and urged the development of a more universally applicable withdrawal scheme. They argued that, if the church's educational aim was to train children to become members of a worshipping community, neither the biblical teaching of the agreed syllabus, nor parental and Sunday school teaching would be sufficient. It was accordingly proposed that a resolution encapsulating these views be forwarded to the president of the Board of Education and to the Archbishop of Canterbury. Richard Brook strongly opposed this line and forced the withdrawal of the resolution.

Possibly as a result of the difference of opinion between the diocesan bishop and the diocesan education committee, the debate about the relative merits of aided and controlled status assumes a low profile in the diocesan education committee's agenda over the next few years. By this time, key educational decisions seemed to have been firmly in the hands of the diocesan bishop. The next that was heard about this question was when Richard Brook issued a policy statement on the subject to the Diocesan Conference in 1947. Referring to the option of aided status he remarked that:

> This will be a very costly matter and in most cases beyond the resources of the Managers. In such cases the schools will have to become controlled schools and all costs fall on the local authority .... It is my conviction that so far as Religious Education is concerned it is neither buildings, syllabuses, nor timetables that matter most. What matters is that the teachers in all the schools whether voluntary or county shall be Christian men and women.

Meanwhile, the development plans drawn up by the local education authorities were proposing to close a significant proportion of the church schools. Of the 105 voluntary schools in their area, the West Suffolk local education authority proposed the eventual closure of 41 (39%). Of the 92 voluntary schools in the area of the East Suffolk local education authority and within the diocese of St Edmundsbury and Ipswich, the development plan envisaged the eventual closure of 38 (41%). Moreover, the diocesan education committee recognised that not all of the voluntary schools earmarked for retention in the development plan would necessarily remain voluntary schools. The diocesan education committee meeting of April 1946 records that "some would become county schools if they were unable to achieve 'aided' status owing to the ministry's decision that a new school on a new site amalgamating two or more existing voluntary schools cannot be 'controlled'".

The diocesan bishop's next move was to encourage the diocesan education committee to draw up a priority list of church schools to be recommended for aided status. The minutes of the diocesan education committee for April 1948 record:

> The Chairman advocated very strongly that the Committee should draw up a list of 'Key' Schools which it thought should be Aided. These should, to a great extent, be Town Schools, or schools drawing children from a large area. The Managers of these Schools should be advised that they could rely on Diocesan help and should apply for Aided Status. All other Voluntary Schools would have to be Controlled unless they could become Aided out of their own resources. He was certain that in country parishes, with a good incumbent, Controlled Schools had a great many advantages.

The bishop's statement, with its implication that diocesan funds would not be provided to help schools to achieve aided status no doubt considerably influenced the decisions made by individual trustees and managers. It was certainly true that many of them were presented with demands for substantial expenditure to secure the remodelling or replacement of their schools. Faced with such pressures no less than twenty schools had closed in the three years between 1947 and 1949. Three-quarters of the remaining schools opted for controlled status, and the proportion which initially had become aided declined as the expenses they incurred became too great for the trustees to meet. Once the majority of schools had become controlled, and therefore the responsibility of the local authorities, a large number of the projected schemes of improvement were abandoned.

Within a very few years the loss of influence sustained by the church became apparent. Roy Southwell became assistant director of education in 1956 and director in 1959. He was keen to make the fullest possible use of controlled status, and even seems to have encouraged incumbents to exceed their rights, confident in the leniency of the local authorities. So confident was he indeed, that when in 1965 one of Her Majesty's Inspectors of schools found doctrinal teaching being given by incumbents to full classes without parental request in several controlled primary schools in West Suffolk, he made a spirited defence to the chief education officer, and raised the matter with the secretary to the schools committee of the Church of England Board of Education. Needless to say, his defence did not prove acceptable to either authority.

Secondary provision: Debenham and Bury St Edmunds

The question of the provision of church secondary schools goes back to a consideration of the recommendations of the Hadow report. The problem for the diocese was, as always, one of finding the capital to invest in its educational enterprise. A church struggling to maintain its involvement in the provision of existing elementary schools was not in a strong position to rise to the challenge of providing new places for secondary education. After very long debate, the diocesan board of education passed the following resolution at its meeting in April 1935.

(1) That the Board of Education takes an active part in the establishment of church area schools.
(2) That such efforts as the Board of Education is able to make in this matter be spread over a number of years and that each year what is possible

be done at appropriate places in close co-operation with the Local Education Authority concerned.

(3) That (subject to the approval of the Board of Finance on financial grounds, such approval or otherwise be given at its meeting on July 18th next) the Board of Education asks Conference to place at its disposal for 1935 a further sum of money not exceeding £505. Such money to be spent as grants in aid to encourage managers of church schools to establish church area schools.

The 1936 Education Act made the church's task of providing places for secondary education considerably easier by empowering local education authorities to make grants of 50–75% towards the cost of building voluntary schools made necessary by the state's declared intention to raise the school leaving age to fifteen on 1 September 1939. However, even this offer of state subsidy left the diocese with a financial burden it could not carry. In the event, only one group of managers in the diocese felt in a position to negotiate this 'special agreement' status with the local education authority for the erection of a church secondary school. These were the managers of the Sir Robert Hitcham school in Debenham. It is from this point that the saga of the Debenham church secondary school begins.

Progress on the development of the special agreement school at Debenham was necessarily halted by the outbreak of the Second World War in 1939. After the war, the diocesan education committee resolved at its meeting in March 1944 to write to the managers of the Sir Robert Hitcham school, Debenham, to tell them that "the committee were of the opinion that it was desirable that the proposals made in 1936 should stand, and that the managers might rely upon the help and support of the committee in endeavouring to give effect to them". From this point onwards, the diocesan education committee became more cautious of the actual cost of supporting this resolution.

At their meeting in June 1946, the estimates prepared by the county architect were presented to the diocesan education committee. The cost of the proposed school was estimated at this time "to be about £78,000 if the county had to build a new school and £62,000 if the managers decided to adapt the present building". After debate "it was generally agreed that it was most desirable that the scheme for a special agreement secondary school at Debenham should go through". The point was stressed in the debate that "this would be the only church secondary school in the diocese and it would serve 18 parishes".

However, when the diocesan education committee proceeded at this meeting to examine its financial resources more closely, the diocesan bishop continued to press for the first priority to be the church training colleges, and "he felt inclined to put the proposed special agreement school at Debenham as the second priority". By September 1947, the diocesan bishop had come to the decision that the cost of keeping Debenham as a special agreement secondary school,

> was likely to be so great that there would be no money left over for any other aided schools. After some discussion it was felt unwise to put all the diocesan resources into one school which could serve only a comparatively small area. The Chairman put the motion to the meeting that Debenham should be a primary aided school instead of a secondary aided school. A vote was taken and the motion was carried.

The idea of developing Sir Robert Hitcham's school in Debenham as an aided primary school went ahead, but the hopes for a church secondary school in the parish were not finally abandoned. In 1955 the diocesan education committee again found itself debating the development of this new secondary school. By 1955 the estimated cost to the church of special agreement status was £21,000. Now the diocesan education committee decided that special agreement status "was not very different from controlled status" and "offered no real advantage". The decision was subsequently taken to develop a church controlled secondary school in Debenham, and this school was finally opened in 1964.

While the addition of a church controlled secondary school in Debenham to the diocese had been the result of conscious planning over a period of twenty-eight years, the acquisition of a church controlled grammar school in Bury St Edmunds seems to have come about more by accident than design. King Edward IV Grammar School in Bury St Edmunds was an ancient foundation. Under the terms of the 1944 Education Act, the governors of this school worked independently of the diocese to acquire controlled status. By reason of the nature of the trust deeds, the Minister of Education favoured the inclusion of this foundation as a church controlled school. A long battle ensued, with the provost of the cathedral being the school governor who acted as the key protagonist for keeping the school independent of the diocesan education committee.

After King Edward IV Grammar School had been constituted as a church controlled school, its relationships with the church continued to be strained, or at the best weak. A long correspondence ensued about the future of the endowments of the school, the governors being most unwilling to hand them over to the diocesan education committee. For its part, the diocesan education committee seemed to have considerable difficulty in appointing a second foundation governor who would take an active interest in the school. The Dean of Bocking, who was appointed by the diocesan education committee for the initial three formative years from 1949 to 1952, attended none of the thirteen meetings of the governing body convened during that period. In 1952 the Dean of Bocking was replaced by Lieut. Col. Sir George Falconer, who attended seven of the eighteen meetings during his five year period in office. He was replaced in 1957 by the Archdeacon of Sudbury, who attended fourteen of the next twenty-nine meetings. In 1962 the other foundation governor appointed by the church, the Revd J.R.M. Wright, confirmed that there had never been reserved teachers or any form of distinctive Church of England teaching given in the school.

Secondary provision: Ipswich

The third place in the diocese to attract discussion about the establishment of a post-primary church school is the borough of Ipswich itself. The three church primary schools in Ipswich all opted for aided status after the 1944 Education Act. Inevitably, the Ipswich church school's association which represented the interests of these three aided schools spotted the inconsistency of maintaining three aided primary schools when these schools were unable to feed into a church secondary school. The file on the proposed secondary school for Ipswich is one of the saddest documents in the archives of the Diocesan Education Office. It demonstrates unambiguously the inability of the diocese to act decisively and powerfully in the educational arena.

The first record of the diocesan education committee's views on a church secondary school in Ipswich is in the minute book for July 1955 when the decision was taken that such a development was not feasible. The Ipswich church schools association was not deterred by this decision, and when the 1959 Education Act created a more favourable climate for the building of new aided secondary schools, the association immediately submitted a new resolution to the diocesan education committee in December 1959, "that the diocesan education committee be urged to take steps to obtain sanction for the building of a church secondary modern school to serve the town of Ipswich". This time the diocesan education committee agreed to the resolution in principle and approached the local education authority. By June 1960, the local education authority had agreed in principle. By September 1960, the Minister of Education agreed that there was a *prima facie* case for a three form entry secondary aided school under the terms of the 1959

Education Act. By December 1960, it seemed that the Minister of Education's major works programme implied the beginning of this new school in 1965. But December 1960 remains the highpoint in the story.

Somehow the Roman Catholic church in Ipswich managed to move a little more quickly than the Anglican church. In May 1963 the diocesan education committee learnt that the Roman Catholic authorities had received approval to begin their secondary aided school. This information spurred the diocese on to set in motion its solicitors to acquire a site. The adventurous notion was to acquire the site adjoining the proposed Roman Catholic secondary aided school. In September 1963 co-operation between the Roman Catholic and the Anglican dioceses was such that details for the provision of essential services was being considered jointly by the Roman Catholic and the Church of England architects.

Such progress was made on the Roman Catholic site that its future was secured before the famous government circular 10/65 changed the requirements for secondary education. Saint Alban's Roman Catholic voluntary aided school was opened as a two form entry secondary school in September 1966 with 144 pupils on the roll. At the time of circular 10/65, however, the Anglican school was still at the drawing board stage. Overnight the situation had changed and the diocesan education committee was forced to admit that a proposed school of 300 secondary pupils was no longer "a viable and satisfactory educational unit". In other words, after circular 10/65, a school of this size was no longer likely to receive ministry of education backing. The full implications of circular 10/65 were gradually felt by the diocesan education committee. At their meeting of March 1966, "some were of the opinion that ... it was now quite unrealistic to expect to build anything to fit in with the new national pattern". At the meeting of September 1966, the diocesan education committee considered substituting "two or more new aided primary schools" for the proposed secondary school. At this point a working party was set up, and nothing further was reported about the issue in the diocesan education committee minutes until September 1971.

At their meeting in September 1971, the diocesan education committee agreed to reactivate with the Department of Education and Science the request for a Church of England aided secondary school in Ipswich. It was agreed to submit a three form entry secondary school, catering for the ages between 11 and 16 years. By May 1972, this new proposal had received the support of the local education authority and had been placed in the Department of Education and Science's schools building preliminary list for 1973/4. Once again, in May 1972 the proposed church aided secondary school for Ipswich seemed to have reached a high point.

A year later, however, in mid-1973, the Department of Education and Science revised its estimate of the provision of secondary places for Ipswich and suggested that an aided secondary school could probably only be justified "if the catchment area could be enlarged to take in surrounding areas". The diocesan education committee responded positively to this set back, although it meant both greater expenditure and considering movement from the site next to the Roman Catholic school to a larger site. In September 1973 the diocesan education committee submitted a revised proposal to permit a five form entry school "which would be more acceptable to the Department of Education and Science".

In 1965, just as progress was being made on the drawing board, the diocesan education committee had seen its hopes of actually building a church secondary school in Ipswich dashed by the government's reorganisation of secondary education. In 1974, as progress was once again being made on the drawing board, the diocesan education committee again saw its hopes dashed, this time by the central government's reorganisation of local government. The borough of Ipswich local education authority, with whom negotiations had been undertaken, suddenly ceased to exist. In January 1975 the diocesan education committee tried to safeguard the future of its proposed secondary school by writing to the chief education officer of the Ipswich borough to seek "a written undertaking that, whenever it becomes possible to consider extra secondary places in the town, discussion will be held with the Church of England representatives at the earliest moment". The chief education officer replied that, given local government reorganisation, it would be difficult to commit his successors, so no such assurance could be given.

Meanwhile, the diocesan education committee also considered the possibility of co-operating with the Roman Catholic church in developing a joint Roman Catholic/Anglican secondary school. The Roman Catholic Bishop of Elmham was not impressed by the idea. In 1977, when the new Roman Catholic diocese of East Anglia was created, the diocesan education committee thought it worthwhile to approach the new bishop of this diocese. The new Bishop of East Anglia replied that he could "foresee many difficulties on all sides". By this time, the Roman Catholic secondary school had become well established in the town and ecumenical experimentation might well have threatened its future development.

In June 1979 the diocesan education committee again decided to write to the county education authority requesting the authority to include a church aided secondary school in its building programme for Ipswich as soon as possible. By this time, however, the local education authority had become aware of the implications of falling school rolls for secondary school places. Not only did the local education authority resist the request to hasten the building of a new church school, it pointed out quite firmly that it could not envisage the need for any further school places in Ipswich in the forseeable future. Having been reminded of the proposed church secondary school for Ipswich, the secondary school sub-committee of the local education authority recommended that the site be disposed of as surplus to foreseeable requirements. The site had originally been bought by the local education authority with the notion of selling part to the diocese at the appropriate time, but the diocese had never completed the transaction. At this point, November 1979, the diocesan education committee recognised its insecurity and asked the local education authority to retain just sufficient of the site for a joint project with the neighbouring Roman Catholic school to be possible at some future date.

The file on the proposed church secondary school for Ipswich ends on this uncertain note of the diocesan education committee's request to the local education authority. No record is available of the local education authority's reply. However, the sale of the whole site was completed on 15 September 1982. After thirty years of prolonged discussion, the Anglican church was no closer to being able to establish a secondary school in Ipswich into which its three primary aided schools could sensibly feed.

New primary provision

As far as its provision of primary school places is concerned, since 1944 the diocesan education committee has tended to think in terms of preserving, improving and extending existing schools where this is feasible, but not in terms of developing new schools. Significant population movements have, however, taken place in the diocese during the period since 1944. Although the diocesan education committee has had no central policy for the consideration of the need for new church primary schools in the areas undergoing population expansion, a few incumbents have spotted the needs for new school places and the advantages to be gained by encouraging the church to develop new primary schools. Just two incumbents were sufficiently persistent to get their initiatives minuted and responded to by the diocesan education committee, but in both cases the slowness of the administrative system successfully killed off local initiative.

In 1968 the Revd Roger Taylor was inducted into the expanding parish of St Peter and St Paul, Felixstowe. The new development in the parish was already well under way, and so within a few months of his arrival in the parish Mr Taylor decided to write to the diocesan education committee: "There must be envisaged a new school here. Do you know whether it is too late for such to be a church school of aided status?" The diocesan director replied almost by return of post, "I do appreciate your desire for the church to maintain her stake in education but I think the diocese is already fully committed in other areas to consider the possibility of pioneer work in Felixstowe".

The parochial church council of St Peter and St Paul's gave serious discussion to the diocesan education committee's reply and accepted that, if finance was the main problem, the only appropriate response was for the local church to take seriously its responsibility for finding the money. However, the parochial church council was far from sure how to proceed with negotiations with the local education authority. They passed a resolution in April 1969 to demonstrate their commitment to the project and instructed their chairman to write again to the diocesan education committee both to convey the resolution that "this council would seriously consider its responsibilities towards finding the required monies" and to seek advice on the next step. This time, the diocesan director of education replied that the matter could not be dealt with until the diocesan education committee had discussed the issue. Five months later, Mr Taylor wrote again to enquire whether the diocesan education committee had yet decided how to respond to his parish's request for advice.

When the diocesan education committee debated the issue, it was decided that a church school for Felixstowe could be considered, but not until the 1977/8 programme. Meanwhile, the need for primary school places was an urgent one and a new county school was opened in the parish. When eventually the local education authority was approached with the request to consider the development of a church aided school, the local education authority replied that there was no need for further primary school provision in the area.

The second parish to consider the development of a new church aided primary school was St Mary Stoke, Ipswich. Here the development of a large new housing area on the estate formerly owned by Lord Belstead had already prompted the diocese to negotiate a site for a new church centre. The rector, the Revd Robert Godfrey, spotted the potential for a church primary school and approached the bishop directly in 1967 to discuss the possibility of developing an aided primary school on the site next to the proposed church centre.

The diocesan education committee responded quickly and favourably to this initiative and instructed the diocesan director of education to write to the chief education officer to request a site. The Chief Education Officer replied cautiously and discouragingly in a letter dated 21 December 1967:

> It is difficult for me to venture an opinion as to whether or not the diocesan education committee should promote a scheme for the provision of a Church of England primary school in this area, particularly as I have no indication of the likely number of children for whom parents would want primary education in a Church of England school.
>
> Having regard to the proposed primary provision by the local education authority in the area, your committee will doubtless wish to consider most carefully whether they should go ahead with the scheme, particularly bearing in the mind the question of finding a suitable site in an appropriate location.

Meanwhile, the rector of St Mary Stoke and the diocesan education committee both proceeded with the project. The rector conducted a survey in the parish to demonstrate the level of public support for the school. The diocese negotiated the opportunity to purchase a site at half its current market value. Plans were discussed for developing a joint church/school site as a multi-use building, making full use of the 80% grant from the Department of Education and Science and the Church Commissioners' allocation for a new housing area. Only delays over the outline planning permission seemed to stand in the way of contracts being exchanged for the site of the first church primary school to be built in the diocese since 1944.

At this point, however, a new problem emerged. In 1971 a notice appeared in the local press indicating that the local education authority was proposing a new county school for that estate. The diocesan education committee naturally protested to the local education authority and sought an explanation as to why its request for a church school had been ignored. The local education authority replied by informing the diocesan education committee that it had never formerly requested the local education authority to provide a site for a church school; in fact, no reply had been received from the diocese to their letter of 21 December 1967. The problem was that in December 1967 the post of diocesan director of education had been vacant in the diocese of St Edmundsbury and Ipswich and inadequate measures had been taken to cover the duties of that office. Through this administrative oversight, the diocese forfeited what might have been a strategically important addition to its pastoral and educational response to the development of a large new housing estate.

Reorganisation

In 1965 the government issued its famous circular 10/65 on the reorganisation of secular education. We have already seen how this circular had a profound impact on the diocese's proposals for a church secondary modern school in Ipswich. The implications of the circular were, of course, widespread throughout the diocese.

The first meeting of the diocesan education committee to discuss the implications of circular 10/65, held in September 1965, fully appreciated the difficulties which the Church of England would face when confronted by such radical proposals for educational reorganisation. The minutes noted tersely "the position of the Church of England was most uncertain, there being no money to implement proposals". The diocesan education committee felt that its only contribution at this stage could be to express the hope "that in the course of time the way forward for all concerned with secondary education would become plain". At the following meeting in November 1965 things had become no plainer, and the minutes record that the situation remained "mainly obscure". If anything, it seems that by March 1966 things might have been becoming worse, with the minutes recording that "the way forward was still most obscure".

When illumination came in September 1966, it came by means of the decisions of the local education authorities concerned. By this time, both East and West Suffolk had proposed responding to circular 10/65 by the development of a three tier system of education, with the introduction of middle schools. On the negative side, the diocesan education committee noted that these proposals would result in the "decapitation of all primary schools and the closure of many". On the more positive side, the hope was expressed that the diocese would have the opportunities for engagement in the middle school provision. Nearly a year later, June 1967, the diocesan education committee noted with relief that "fortunately no immediate decisions were required".

The diocesan education committee continued to give careful thought to the implications of reorganisation on the basis of the three tier system. On several occasions the chief education officers of the East and West Suffolk authorities attended the meetings of the diocesan education committee to state the positions of their respective authorities. The diocesan education committee then passed the following resolution in October 1968.

The St Edmundsbury and Ipswich diocesan education committee welcomes the opportunities which secondary reorganisation will bring to the church within the counties of East Suffolk and West Suffolk and the county borough of Ipswich. They pledge themselves to co-operate in the practical application of the various schemes and state their desire to participate in all sectors of education, including middle schools, where applicable.

The plans for reorganisation moved more quickly in West Suffolk than in East Suffolk. In March 1970 the diocesan education committee submitted to the West Suffolk local education authority proposals for one aided middle school in Bury St Edmunds and for seven controlled middle schools in Beyton, Bury St Edmunds, Hadleigh, Ixworth, Mildenhall, Sudbury and Newmarket. What was agreed with the local education authority was the aided middle school in Bury St Edmunds and four controlled middle schools in Sudbury, Mildenhall, Newmarket and Stanton. The Mildenhall school was not built, but the other three controlled and the one aided school were built.

During the 1970s, the three tier system was totally implemented in West Suffolk. While the diocese gained four middle schools, at the same time it lost the third and fourth year junior pupils from its primary schools. Inevitably this decapitation of the smaller church primary schools resulted in some closures. At the end of the 1970s, the diocese was left in the former administrative area of West Suffolk with a total of 58 first schools, 4 middle schools and an upper school, resulting from the redesignation of the King Edward IV Grammar School in Bury St Edmunds as a church controlled upper school.

In East Suffolk, the reorganisation on the three tier system did not progress as thoroughly as in West Suffolk. In East Suffolk, the diocese developed a middle school at Butley. Some of its primary schools were retained as five through eleven year schools, while others became first schools. The secondary modern school at Debenham became an eleven through sixteen comprehensive school.

While the local education authorities were busy reorganising the provision for state maintained schools within the diocese, the diocese itself became busy reorganising the work of its education committee and staff. It seems clear that the diocese, perhaps among other concerns, had become alarmed by the prospect of incurring large capital costs in pursuit of maintaining its educational involvement in schools upon reorganisation. In 1972 the diocesan commission on needs and resources included among its recommendations that consideration should be given to the question whether the retention of aided status for isolated schools could be justified; that the education committee should incur no further debts until a policy for the deployment of resources in the field of education as a whole, including youth work, had been formulated; and that an urgent reappraisal of its work and structures be expressed in terms of greater efficiency and co-operation within its departments.

At this stage the diocesan director of education resigned. The diocesan synod then set up a working party on education. In its report the working party made it clear that it considered the education of adult members of the church as being the prime need of the diocese, and quoted the Carlisle Report on the importance of working to achieve "... a genuine freeing of adults for responsible, informed, articulate living in a world where the truth of the Christian religion is in question." To this end it recommended the establishment of an education team, one member of which was to be a schools officer so as to free the director from being "excessively preoccupied with schools work". The emphasis on adult education at the expense of involvement with church schools was further reinforced by the fact that the new director, when appointed, combined his directorship with the post of adult education officer. The work envisaged for the specialist schools officer was seen to be of a primarily administrative and financial nature, and was performed together with parochial duties. A youth officer and a religious education adviser for Sunday schools and day schools were to complete the team.

This reorganisation set the scene for the diocese to adopt a low profile on the church school front throughout the rest of the 1970s. The diocesan education committee decided to delegate much of its work in the area of church schools to the school sub-committee, while after October 1975 the school sub-committee met for only a total of three meetings during the next six years.

The small school question

In 1980 the school sub-committee was brought suddenly back into life. After the recent history of infrequent meetings, the committee found itself convened seven times in the space of twelve months between

September 1980 and September 1981. The main agenda item for the first of this new cycle of meetings in September 1980 was the 'Future of Small Schools'.

By September 1980 falling rolls and increasing financial stringency were encouraging the local education authority to review the future of certain small schools. Included on the list for review were five Church of England schools. Local education authority projections were predicting that by 1984 rolls would have fallen to 20 at Wattisfield and Stoke by Clare, to 25 at Hepworth and Wetherden and to 30 at Parham.

After debating and assessing the arguments for and against the closure of small schools, the school sub-committee recommended the retention of four of the five schools under review, recommending the closure only of Parham. Two months later the local education authority primary sub-committee recommended the closure of four of the five schools, recommending the retention only of Stoke by Clare. Just as the scene seemed set for a battle of opinion between the diocesan education committee and the local education authority, the Suffolk County Council ignored the recommendations of both committees and decided against the immediate closure of any small schools.

The alternative proposal put forward by the county council was the notion of reducing the staffing level of these schools to one full-time and one half-time teacher and introducing a 'self-help scheme' from September 1981, in the hope that there would be some financial support from the local community to subsidise the running of uneconomic units. The proposal was for a trial five year period, with a review after three years. Four of the five schools entered the self-help scheme, while numbers in the fifth school rose sufficiently to make this move unnecessary. Three years later, at the time of the review, the primary education sub-committee came to the conclusion that, in spite of "the considerable efforts made in difficult circumstances", all four of these schools were no longer "viable either in educational or financial terms". As a consequence of this decision, the aided school at Parham and the controlled schools at Wetherdon, Wattisfield and Stoke by Clare are scheduled for closure in July 1986.

A different kind of problem emerged for the diocesan education committee when, in January 1982, the local education authority proposed the closure of the two controlled schools at Mellis and Gislingham and their replacement by a new school at Gislingham. This proposal resulted in considerable local controversy. Eventually the Secretary of State did not allow the county council to discontinue Mellis school and, as a consequence, the county council decided not to proceed with the building of a new school at Gislingham. The problem of these two small schools remains to be fought at another time.

In the autumn of 1981, the local education authority adopted a policy designed to take a more strategic approach to the problem of surplus school places. Instead of waiting for rolls to fall in individual schools and reviewing their future when they fell below a certain threshold, the local education authority initiated a new process of 'area reviews'. The aim of the area review is to rationalise educational provision throughout the county by examining logically coherent areas one by one, based on secondary school catchment areas. Preliminary prediction by the local education authority suggested the need for the removal of 5,500 surplus primary places, with the possible closure of up to 35 of the 282 primary schools in Suffolk over ten years or so.

Such a process of area reviews highlights the added complexities created by the dual system of voluntary and county schools in achieving unified educational provision. The process inevitably sharpens the churches' perceptions of their partnership with the state in the provision of schools. The diocesan education committee quickly accepted its responsibility to be involved in this educational debate over rationalisation and convened an extraordinary meeting in March 1982. Considerable effort was put into collecting information for this meeting, involving the presentation of five papers, including a theological view from the diocesan director of education, an educational view from the assistant local education officer and an economic view from the diocesan schools officer. As a result of the extraordinary meeting, the diocesan education committee resolved to "undertake consultations with local communities over the full implications of closure proposals", and to set up a working party "to produce guidelines for the diocesan education committee's helping communities to face closure constructively".

The actual process of area reviews was initiated in 1983. The reviews in the Sudbury and Haverhill areas were relatively painless for the diocesan education committee. The Sudbury review did not recommend the closure of any church schools, but advocated that both the controlled middle and a controlled primary school should move to new sites. The Haverhill review included no Church of England schools within its area.

The reviews in the Stowupland and Woodbridge areas were more painful for the diocesan education committee. The Stowupland review proposed the closure of three controlled schools at Finningham, Old Newton and Drinkstone. While the local education authority sub-committee reprieved Old Newton, Finningham was closed in 1984 and Drinkstone has the approval of the Secretary of State for closure in 1986. The review in the Woodbridge area recommended the closure of Butley Controlled Middle School, the only Church of England middle school in the whole of East Suffolk. At the same time, Bawdsey Controlled Primary School, while retained on a temporary basis, is scheduled for review after three years.

In this way, the mid-1980s small school question is beginning to have an impact on the church school provision within the diocese. After a decade, between 1974 and 1984, during which the stock of church schools had remained constant, the mid-1980s is once again seeing a slimming down in the voluntary component to the state maintained sector of schools.

3 THE SURVEY

Before looking at what the research project discovered about the perceptions and attitudes of those who teach in church schools, it is necessary to examine in some detail the *method* used in the study. After all, the results of research are no stronger than the methods by which they are obtained. This chapter, therefore, proposes to discuss three central issues, namely the way in which the research grew from and was sponsored by a diocesan working party; the design and preliminary testing of the research questionnaire; and the sampling strategy, including the way in which the questionnaire was distributed and the kind of response it received.

Working party

The original initiative to undertake this research came from within the diocese itself. The diocesan education committee decided that one of its priorities for the current session should be to evaluate the role of church schools in the diocese and to discuss policy for the future. The way through which the diocesan education committee decided to further these aims was by setting up a working party, known in the diocese as the 'church schools working party'.

The composition of the working party was a crucial matter. The aim was to bring together a range of expertise and points of view without producing a body of unwieldy size. The nine people appointed to the working party included the diocesan religious education adviser, the diocesan schools officer, the headmaster of a Church of England voluntary aided primary school who was also a member of the National Union of Teachers, the headmistress of a Church of England voluntary aided primary school who was also a member of the National Association of Headteachers, the headmaster of a Church of England voluntary controlled secondary school who was also chairman of the diocesan education committee, the rector of a group of rural parishes who was also chairman of the governors of a church school, a lay member of the diocesan education committee, the assistant county education officer, and myself as a non-stipendiary parish priest, a governor of a church school and educational researcher.

The first task of the working party was to assemble as much information about the church schools in the diocese as possible and to identify the additional information which would be helpful in evaluating the present situation and in formulating policy. The working party raised questions about the distinctiveness of church schools, that is to say about the ways in which church schools differ from county schools, if at all. We wanted to find a way in which we could get hold of those elusive notions that people have about the differences between church schools and county schools and check whether these notions have any substance in reality. Each member of the working party had his or her own views to contribute on this question, but none of us could support our opinions with anything more solid that anecdotes about the schools we knew best; and some of our anecdotes clearly contradicted each other.

Time and time again attention was focused on the importance of the teaching staff in determining whether there were any differences between church schools and county schools or not. We realised that the finest policy statements, formulated at national, diocesan, or even local level, about the distinctiveness of church schools were ultimately secondary to the views and dispositions of the teaching staff in whose hands the actual day to day running of the schools rested. As far as we could discover, no diocese had tried to assemble systematic information about the attitudes and perceptions of those who teach in Church of England voluntary aided and voluntary controlled schools. This aim, then, became a priority of the working party and gave birth to the present research project.

The only ways to discover the information which the working party needed about the attitudes and perceptions of the teachers in church schools inevitably involved making some direct approach to the teachers themselves. The working party was sure that, if the teachers in church schools were to be approached in this kind of way, they should also be assured that the results of the research would become quickly available to them. As part of the design of the research project the working party committed itself to making the results available to the biennial meeting arranged in the diocese for the headteachers of church schools.

The sponsorship of the research by the diocesan education committee, the careful composition of the working party and the agreement that the results of the research would be shared with the biennial conference of church school headteachers are three important factors in establishing the status of the research project among the schools who were invited to co-operate with it. The research project was seen to have much more than simply a theoretical or academic function. The project was clearly of importance to the diocesan education committee and to the staff members of the diocesan education office; it was clear that church school teachers were themselves closely involved in the design of the project; it was clear that the local education authority was fully cognizant of the project; it was clear that members of at least two unions were represented on the working party; it was clear that a professional educational researcher was involved in the project; it was clear that the results of the research would come back to the church schools and the diocese. Against this carefully prepared background, the research project was able to explore a number of sensitive issues in depth.

Questionnaire

It is one thing for a working party to decide that it would be valuable to learn about the attitudes and perceptions of those who teach in church schools: it is a completely different matter to know how to get hold of this information. There are two basic ways in which social researchers can go about the job of listening to the attitudes and perceptions of a group of people. Some researchers prefer to use interviews, while others prefer to use questionnaires. In trying to choose between these two methods there is a lot to be said on either side.

Two main snags with the interview method are that it takes a lot of time and is expensive to put into practice. The working party realised that it was not in a position to fund a full-time interviewer to drive round to all the schools in the diocese and to spend perhaps an hour or more with each teacher. So on practical grounds this method was ruled out.

Two main snags with the questionnaire method are that some people feel that questionnaires can be too impersonal and that others feel that questionnaires fail to give people scope to express the true range of their feelings. However, the design and use of questionnaires for the measurement of attitudes has become a very sophisticated and highly developed branch of social research in its own right with a respectable history going back over half a century. Given the right amount of thought and care at the design stage, it is possible to overcome these two difficulties.

The first objection to questionnaires, the one concerned with the feeling that they are impersonal, is a problem which can be largely overcome by making the administration of the questionnaire as personal as possible. The working party resolved that, if it was to use a questionnaire, it would not simply send the questionnaire out to the teachers by post. Each school would be visited personally and the whole matter of the research project would be talked through with the headteacher or with the whole staff. The diocesan religious education adviser took on the bulk of this work in the course of her contacts with schools, while other members of the working party assisted in the task where appropriate.

The second objection to questionnaires, the one concerned with the feeling that they fail to tap the real range of the attitudes held by different people, is a problem which can be minimised by careful professional design. So it is to this question of the design of the questionnaire that we ought next to turn our attention.

There are two main styles of questionnaire that can be used. The first style uses 'open-ended' questions which would require the teachers to write in their own answers. What makes this style so unsatisfactory are three problems. First, they take a lot of time for the teacher to complete since each question requires detailed thought. In fact, some would say that this kind of questionnaire actually transfers the real hardwork from the person who designs it to those who have to decide how to fill it in. Second, some people are bound to give more time and care to their answers than others. At the end of the day with this method the researcher never knows whether the shorter answers are short because the teacher has nothing more to say on the subject or because he or she cannot be bothered to say it. Third, the researcher has an enormous problem in knowing what to do with all the answers when they are returned. It is like having to distil a coherent picture from a large number of individual essays.

The second main style of questionnaire is the 'closed-response' type. This means that every question in the questionnaire is carefully thought out beforehand and that the teacher is given a definite and limited range of answers to choose from. With this type of questionnaire, the researcher can derive only a limited amount of information from the answers to each question. The skill in designing this type of questionnaire lies in the ability to devise a wide range of interrelated questions. A great deal of exact and detailed information about the teachers' attitudes can then be constructed from a careful analysis not only of the answers to individual questions but of the pattern that emerges from the answers to a range of questions. In the professional language of the social researcher, the design of this type of questionnaire is known as 'attitude scaling', and some very sophisticated statistical techniques have been developed to make this task as thorough and as foolproof as possible.

The sort of questionnaire developed by the present research project is the 'closed-response' type. The two forms of closed-response question employed are 'multiple-choice' and 'Likert'. The multiple-choice format asks the respondents to choose from a range of pre-coded answers and to place a tick against the correct or the most appropriate answer. The Likert format asks the respondents to rate their responses on a form of scale, for example, a five point scale ranging from 'agree strongly', through 'agree', 'not certain' and 'disagree' to 'disagree strongly'.

The first step in designing a sensible questionnaire is to become clear precisely what it is that the questionnaire wishes to discover. The working party defined four main areas, namely information about the personal background of the teachers, about their attitudes towards the church school system, about their perceptions of what church schools ought to be doing, and about their perceptions of the ways in which church schools do or do not differ from county schools.

The second step was for the working party to talk in depth about the precise questions which would define the four areas of content. After listening to what each of the members of the working party had to say about these areas, as the professional researcher on the working party, I translated their intentions into a draft form of the questionnaire. The next meeting of the working party subjected the draft questionnaire to a full and exhaustive critique. A second draft was produced. The two headteachers of Church of England voluntary aided primary schools on the working party asked their staff to complete the second draft of the questionnaire. These two headteachers held a full discussion with their staff about their reactions to the questionnaire. These reactions were brought back to the working party, leading to the third and final draft of the questionnaire.

This process of development, involving both frequent interchange between the professional researcher and the members of the working party and also a small pilot testing in two schools, improved the quality of the questionnaire greatly. The final version of the questionnaire contained four main sections.

Part one of the questionnaire is concerned with collecting background information. We wanted to know as much as possible about the kind of people who teach in the church schools in the diocese. How many men teachers and how many women teachers are there in the schools? How are the headships and other posts of responsibility shared among the sexes? How old are the teachers, and what is the average age of those in charge of the schools?

Do those who teach in church schools tend to live in the community served by their schools? Are they practising members of a Christian Church, and, if so, is this necessarily the Church of England? Do the teachers who attend church make a point of going to the church with which their school is historically associated so that they may find themselves worshipping alongside the children who attend their school and the parents of those children?

Have those who are teaching in church schools generally set out to select for themselves a post in a denominational voluntary school, or is it just a matter of chance that they find themselves in a church school? If they had the complete freedom to choose the type of school in which they taught would they prefer to opt for a Church of England aided, a Church of England controlled, a Roman Catholic aided, a county, or an independent school? To what extent have those who are now teaching in Church of England schools had the experience of teaching in other types of school? For example, how many teachers in Church of England schools have ever held a teaching post in a Roman Catholic school?

The final aim of the first part of the questionnaire is to glean an overall indication of the commitment of those who teach in church schools to the voluntary component within the state maintained sector of education, and an overall impression of their understanding of the function of this voluntary component.

Part two of the questionnaire is concerned with analysing the teachers' attitudes to the church school system as they know and experience it in practice. This part of the questionnaire is concerned with much more than producing an overall indication of whether those who teach in church schools are in favour of the system or not. It sets out to listen to the teachers' assessment of nine key aspects of their experience of church schools.

First, we examine their views of what it means to teach in a church school. To what extent is teaching in a church school seen as being different from teaching in a county school? Do they have any particular views about the kind of people who are best suited for teaching in church schools? Do they reckon that teachers should receive any special initial or in-service training to equip them for working in church schools? Do they reckon that the teaching of religious education is a matter of particular concern in church schools and one that requires specific qualifications or qualities?

Second, we turn attention to the views which the teachers have on admission policies. Do they reckon that Church of England schools should concentrate on providing places for the children of practising Anglicans, or for the children of practising Christian parents irrespective of their denomination, or for all children of the neighbourhood in exactly the same way as county schools? Should Church of England schools set out to provide an alternative place of education for Anglicans in a similar way to that in which Roman Catholic schools provide an alternative place for Catholics? Should Church of England schools concentrate on helping children with special needs, irrespective of their religious background or lack of it?

Third, we look at the way in which those who teach in church schools envisage the future of their schools developing. How many of them regard Church of England schools as having outlived their usefulness? How many would like to see the Church of England hand over its church schools to the state? How many feel that at least there should be a reduction in the number of church schools? How many feel that the Church of England can no longer afford its church schools? On the other hand, how many believe that the Church of England should try to expand its stake in church schools, especially at the level of secondary, middle or upper schools where its stake is at present the smallest? How many would like to support the development of interdenominational schools? How do they regard the way in which the Roman Catholic Church runs its church schools?

Fourth, we try to quantify the extent to which teachers in church schools are critical of the effects of voluntary schools either on the children who attend them or on society at large. To what extent do the teachers regard church schools as socially or racially divisive? To what extent do they consider that church schools give an unfair privilege to some children, or indeed to Christian teachers in the promotion stakes? To what extent would they go along with the criticism that church schools tend to alienate pupils from the church or help to turn children away from Christianity?

Fifth, the accelerated secularisation of society in general and of education in particular during the 1970s has caused educational theorists increasingly to question the close ties between education and religion apparently assumed at the time of the 1944 Education Act. To what extent are those who teach in church schools reflecting this change in the climate of educational theory? What proportion of teachers in church schools want to stress that it is not a legitimate aim either of county schools or church schools to initiate children into a religious faith? What proportion of teachers in church schools go along with the theory that worship in school assembly should be abandoned? To what extent do teachers in church schools promote the notion that there can be no specifically Christian view of education?

Sixth, we examine their views on the place of religious education in church schools. Do they see the job of religious education in church schools as being in any sense different from that in county schools? How many of them would give their approval to the often quoted aim of religious education in the county school as being "to help children to understand what religion is and what it would mean to take religion seriously"? Do many of them feel that the job of religious education should be taken away from the school and left firmly in the hands of parents and the churches? To what extent do they reckon that church schools have a legitimate mandate to give denominational teaching, and, if so, what do they think this denominational teaching should involve in a Church of England school? For example, should Church of England schools specifically teach their pupils about the communion service and have communion celebrated in the school?

Seventh, what kind of image have those who teach in church schools of the church which sponsors those schools and of the diocesan education office in particular? Do they feel that the Church of England takes enough interest in its church schools? Do they feel that the diocese gives enough help to church schools? Do they feel that the Church of England does enough to produce curriculum materials for the teaching of religious education in church schools?

Eighth, we turn attention to the way in which the teachers view the local church and the foundation governors which the church appoints to serve the school. Do they feel that the local church takes enough interest in its church schools? Do they feel that the school has the right amount of contact with the local church, with the local clergy, or with the foundation governors? Do they feel that the foundation governors actually understand the role of church schools in today's society? Do they see enough of the foundation governors around the school, and are they pleased to see them when they visit?

Finally, what do teachers in church schools think of the clergy's relationship with the school? Is there any professional rivalry between the qualified teacher and the clergyman? Do teachers in church schools tend to feel that the clergy should keep themselves at a greater distance from the professional concerns of the teacher, or do they welcome the clergy's involvement in the school? How often do teachers find the clergy an embarrassment in the school? Are they inclined to doubt the clergy's professional ability to teach, to take assembly, or to be up to date with educational theory and practice?

Parts three and four of the questionnaire go very closely together. The aim of part three is to identify what the teachers see to be the *characteristics* of Church of England primary schools, while the aim of part four is to identify what they see to be the *distinctiveness* of Church of England primary schools. In other words, part three examines the educational priorities which the teachers hold, while part four examines the extent to which the teachers consider that their priorities are different because they are working in a Church of England school rather than in a county school.

The way in which the questionnaire looks at these two distinct but highly related issues is by presenting the teachers with the same list of educational priorities or goals on two occasions. In part three they are asked to assess how important they think each goal is on a five point scale, ranging from 'very important' through 'quite important', 'quite unimportant' and 'very unimportant' to 'not appropriate'. In part four they are asked to assess how much attention Church of England schools should give to each of the same goals compared with county schools. Again, their rating is on a five point scale, this time ranging from 'much more' through 'little more', 'some' and 'little less' to 'much less'.

In order to provide a thorough description of the teachers' perceptions of both the characteristics and the distinctiveness of church schools, the questionnaire includes items about eight key aspects of school life.

First, we examine their understanding of the curriculum. How do the teachers regard the relative priority they ascribe to teaching different aspects of the curriculum? For example, do they give a higher priority to teaching numeracy or literacy, to teaching social studies or environmental studies, to teaching moral education or religious education? What priority do they give to sex education? How do they rate the importance of teaching music, art or physical education? Do they reckon that the weight given to any of these subjects should be different because they are teaching in a church school?

Second, we give particular attention to the teachers' views on religious education. To what extent do they consider that their school should be teaching Christianity to the pupils, or should they concentrate more on teaching about other world religions? Should religious education be kept as a distinct component on the timetable, or should it be integrated with secular studies? Do they reckon that the kind of religious education given in church schools should be different from that given in state schools?

Third, we look at the idea of whether the school should be regarded as some form of 'Christian community'. To what extent do the teachers feel that it is the job of their schools to provide a Christian assembly on a regular basis, or even every day? Do they feel that their school should 'provide an atmosphere of Christian community', or be a place which puts 'into practice Christian values'? Do they feel that it is important for their school to have committed Christians on the staff? Do they feel that there should be a place for classroom prayers in schools, or for a regular communion service to be celebrated in school? Do they feel that a Church of England school should set out to provide a Christian environment in some sense different from county schools?

Fourth, we review their understanding of the ethos of the school. To what extent do they consider that their school should set out to promote a high level of academic attainment? What priority should the school give to helping the slower pupils, or to being available to counsel individual children with special needs? How important is it that the pupils enjoy their time in school, or feel that they have confidence and trust in the staff? Do the teachers reckon that either the academic standard or the caring environment of a church school should be different from that of a county school?

Fifth, we analyse the teachers' views of the relationship between the school and the local community. What priority do they feel the school should give to developing close contacts with parents, with people from the local community, or with the local clergy? Do they feel that the school should encourage parents to help in the school itself in various ways? Do they feel that the local clergy should be encouraged to visit the school? How much of a responsibility do they feel that the school has to know about the pupils' home background, and to offer advice and help to their parents when they seek it? Do they feel that the links between the school and the local community should be any different in the case of a church school?

Sixth, we examine the views which the teachers hold about the contribution of the school to the moral development of their pupils. To what extent do they regard it as the job of the school to instil traditional moral values into the pupils? Do they reckon that a church school should be any more or less committed to its view of moral development than a county school?

The seventh and eighth areas concern the distinctions made by educationalists between 'traditional' and 'progressive' educational methods. Many of the items adopted to characterise these two areas were derived directly from Neville Bennett's well known study, *Teaching Styles and Pupil Progress*, published by Open Books in 1976. As an indication of traditional methods we look at the priority teachers give to regular spelling tests or maths tests, to learning multiplication tables by heart, to giving stars or other credits for good work, to following a regular timetable, to streaming according to ability, to adopting a firm classroom discipline, and so on. As an indication of progressive methods we look at the decisions to adopt an integrated day, to follow a project approach to learning, to encourage free expression, to allow the children to move around the classroom, to allow the children to decide for themselves where they are going to sit, and generally to talk to one another.

To what extent do the teachers in church schools tend to align themselves with a progressive view of education, and to what extent do they tend to align themselves with a traditional view? Even more significantly, to what extent do they regard their position on the progressive-traditional continuum to be a direct consequence of teaching in a Church of England school?

Sample

Having designed the questionnaire, it was necessary to be clear to whom it was to be distributed and how this distribution was to take place. All told, there were 20 aided and 91 controlled Church of England first, primary and middle schools in the diocese. It was decided to invite all of those who were teaching full-time in these schools to co-operate in the project. In this way, each full-time teacher in a church first, primary or middle school in the diocese would be given an opportunity to make his or her personal views known.

In the 20 aided schools there were a total of 142 full-time teachers. The largest of these schools was the one aided middle school in the diocese with a staff of 25. At the other end of the scale, 5 of the aided first or primary schools had only 2 full-time members of staff each. This means that the other 14 aided schools have an average of 7 or 8 full-time teachers each.

In the 91 controlled schools, there were a total of 377 full-time teachers. The 4 controlled middle schools accounted for 89 of these teachers, an average of 22 each. The majority of the first and primary controlled schools were very small. Four of these schools had just 1 full-time member of staff. Thirty-six of them had 2 full-time teachers; 21

had 3 full-time teachers, and 12 had 4 full-time teachers. This means that the remaining 14 controlled schools had an average of 6 or 7 full-time teachers each, with the largest of these schools having a staff of 17.

The most satisfactory way to sample the whole full-time teaching staff in the church schools in the diocese involved giving a questionnaire to each teacher by name. When the list of teachers was drawn up, each school was given a code number, and each teacher within the school was given a number. These numbers were also written on the top of the questionnaires. The teachers were asked to return their questionnaire to the Culham College Institute in a pre-paid envelope. The questionnaires were returned anonymously and the teachers were assured that the numbers would be torn off as soon as the envelope was opened. This numbering system enabled us to know who had returned the questionnaire and to send some form of reminder after a certain period of time to those who had failed to do so.

Because we believed that it was important for the questionnaires to be distributed personally, they were not sent by post. During the course of one term each school was visited and the purpose of the questionnaire was explained to the headteacher. Wherever possible, the individual teachers were also seen personally. The largest part of this work was undertaken by the diocesan religious education adviser as part of her routine contact with schools, but other members of the working party, the diocesan education team and the diocesan education committee also assisted where appropriate. As a result of this careful strategy a great deal of goodwill, co-operation and interest was generated in the project, although, inevitably, some teachers took an exception to the project for one reason or another.

All told, questionnaires were sent to 519 teachers; 338 of them returned their questionnaires thoroughly and carefully completed. This makes a very satisfactory response rate of 65%. Quite a few more returned partially completed questionnaires, with one or more sections left incomplete. Since it is always difficult to know how to handle partially completed questionnaires, and since the response rate was so good anyway, it was decided to treat partially completed questionnaires as an indication of an unwillingness to co-operate fully in the project. Consequently these partially completed responses were omitted from the final analysis.

The high proportion of the teachers who gave so much of their time and thought to the careful completion of the detailed and lengthy questionnaire is itself a good indication of their interest in the project and their willingness to help in the evaluation of the church school system within the diocese. Interestingly, the teachers in the aided schools showed a higher level of interest in the project than the teachers in the controlled schools: 76% of the teachers in aided schools returned completed questionnaires, in comparison with 60% of those in controlled schools.

It is on the basis of the 338 completed questionnaires that the following chapters are written.

4 THE TEACHERS

Before the subsequent chapters turn attention to an analysis of the views held by those who teach in church schools, the present chapter sets out to discover something about the teachers themselves. Who, in fact, are the people who teach in church schools today? What is the ratio between male and female teachers? How are the headships and other posts of responsibility shared among the sexes? How old are the teachers, and what is the average age of those in charge of the schools?

Do those who teach in Church of England schools claim to be members of a Christian church, and, if so, is this necessarily the Church of England? Is there any difference in the religious affiliation of those who teach in Church of England aided and in Church of England controlled schools? Do they generally claim themselves to be church-goers, and, if so, how frequent are they in their patterns of attendance? Do the teachers who attend church make a point of going to the church with which their school is historically associated so that they may find themselves worshipping alongside the children who attend their school and the parents of those children? Do they live in the community served by their school?

Have those who are teaching in church schools generally set out to select for themselves a post in a denominational voluntary school, or is it often a matter of chance that they find themselves in a church school? If they had the complete freedom to choose the type of school in which they taught would they prefer to opt for a Church of England aided, a Church of England controlled, a Roman Catholic aided, a county, or an independent school? To what extent have those who are now teaching in Church of England schools had experience of teaching in other types of school? Indeed, how committed are those who teach in church schools to the voluntary component within the state maintained sector of education, and what would they like to see the future hold for church schools in general?

Sex

Children who attend a rural church primary school are twice as likely to be taught by a woman than by a man. Overall in the sample of 338 teachers, there were exactly twice as many women (67%) as men (33%). Looking at the two types of church schools separately, a higher proportion of the staff in the controlled schools (37%) are men, compared with the aided schools (27%).

Although considerably more women than men teach in church primary schools in a rural diocese, the higher posts of responsibility tend to be held by male teachers. Of the headteachers in the sample, 63% were men, while of the deputy headteachers, 47% were men. This compares with the fact that 90% of the scale one teachers were women, and 71% of those in scale two or scale three posts were also women. Implicitly or explicitly, church school governors may well still be favouring the appointment of a male headteacher.

Age

Children who attend a rural church primary school are, comparatively speaking, unlikely to be taught by a young teacher straight from college since these schools are generally staffed by more mature teachers. Overall, the ages of those teaching in church schools are fairly evenly distributed over the thirty year age band between the ages of thirty and fifty-nine: 32% of the staff are in their thirties, 27% are in their forties and 26% are in their fifties. Only a very small proportion (4%) are aged sixty years or over. There are also comparatively few (11%) young teachers under the age of thirty. The age structure of those teaching in aided and controlled schools is roughly the same.

The headships of these rural church schools seem to be particularly favoured by teachers in their forties, possibly men and women experiencing their first headship before moving on to a larger school: 29% of the headteachers are men and women aged between thirty and thirty-nine, 37% are aged between forty and forty-nine, and 28% are aged between fifty and fifty-nine. Only 6% of the headteachers are aged sixty years or over. More than half of the deputy headteachers are men and women in their thirties or in their late twenties, while 28% are in their forties and the remaining 17% are in their fifties.

The scale one posts tend to be more evenly distributed over the wider age range of the early twenties to the early sixties: 24% of the scale one posts are held by teachers in their twenties, 25% in their thirties, 24% in their forties, 25% in their fifties and just 2% in their sixties.

Half of the scale two and three posts (48%) have been filled by men and women in their twenties and thirties, who may well be using these posts as stepping off points for further promotion. Another third of these posts (32%) are occupied by those in their fifties or sixties, who may well now be content to stay in these posts until retirement.

Community involvement

When many of the church schools were founded in the nineteenth century, it was often assumed that the teaching staff would live in the community served by the school, and school houses were provided to make this possible. Changes in the patterns of rural life, in the structure of the teaching profession, in the closure and amalgamation of rural schools, and in the ease with which it is possible to travel considerable distances to work have all served to alter the relationship between the rural school teachers and the community in which they work. Few church schools have retained their school houses; very few indeed of these houses are now occupied by the teaching staff.

Nevertheless, in spite of all these changes, a third (33%) of those teaching in church schools still live within the area served by their schools and are therefore able to have a range of day to day contacts not only with their pupils, but also with their parents. Moreover, there is a significantly greater tendency for those teaching in aided schools (43%) to live in the area served by their school than for those teaching in controlled schools (28%).

Those most likely to live in the area served by their schools are the teachers on scale one (37%) or scale two or three (34%) posts. By way of comparison, 28% of the headteachers and 27% of the deputy headteachers live in the area in which they teach. It is likely that those who seek promotion to headships or deputy headships are willing to travel some distance to work, while those who are less ambitious are willing to remain at a more junior level within a school nearer to their existing home.

While a third of the teachers live in the catchment area served by their school, only one-fifth of them (21%) actually live in the parish in which the school is situated.

Church involvement

Two-thirds (68%) of the teachers in church schools in the sample regard themselves as being members of the Church of England. Many of the others regard themselves as belonging to one of the other Christian denominations: 7% are Methodists, 3% are Baptists, 3% are Roman Catholics, 3% belong to the United Reformed Church, and a further 5% belong to other Christian groups. This means that only 11%

of the teachers in rural church primary schools deny all Christian adherence: 4% call themselves agnostic, 3% atheist and 4% humanist. None of the teachers in the sample described themselves as belonging to other world faiths.

There is a greater tendency for those in aided schools (81%) to be members of the Church of England than for those in controlled schools (62%). At the other end of the spectrum, 14% of the teachers in controlled schools claim to be atheists, humanists or agnostics, compared with just 5% of the teachers in aided schools. The governors of aided schools seem to be taking greater care to appoint Christians to their teaching staff.

There is also a greater tendency for those in posts of higher responsibility in church schools to describe themselves as members of the Church of England: 77% of the headteachers are members of the Church of England, compared with 65% of those holding scale one, two or three posts. At the other end of the spectrum, only 2% of the headteachers claim to be atheists, agnostics or humanists compared with 14% of those in scale one, two or three posts. The governors of both aided and controlled schools seem to be taking particular care to appoint members of the Church of England to headships in their rural church schools.

Two-fifths (40%) of the teachers in church schools say that they go to a church service most weeks, and a further 16% say that they go at least once a month. 18% say that they go to the major church festivals although they do not attend church more regularly than this, and a further 12% will attend church perhaps just once in the course of a year. This means that only 12% of those who teach in church schools in the diocese say that they never go to church at all.

Once again, there is a greater tendency towards church-going among those who teach in aided schools: 56% of the teachers in aided schools attend church most weeks, compared with 33% of the teachers in controlled schools. At the other end of the scale, only 2% of those in aided schools say that they never attend church on a Sunday, compared with 18% of those in controlled schools.

Similarly, those who hold headships or deputy headships are more likely to be regular church-goers than those in other teaching posts: 52% of the headteachers and 48% of the deputy headteachers attend church most weeks, compared with 34% of those in other teaching posts.

Although a high proportion of those who teach in church schools are themselves church-goers, more often than not their church association is not with the parish church to which their own school is linked. Only

12% of the teachers would claim to have regular weekly contact with the services in the church associated with their school, while a further 5% have monthly contact with that church. In this sense the relationship between the regular Sunday worship of the parish church and the local church school remains weak.

Again, those who teach in church aided schools are more likely to worship weekly in the parish church associated with their school (22%) than those who teach in church controlled schools (8%). Looked at another way, 51% of those who teach in controlled schools and 40% of those who teach in aided schools never attend Sunday church services in the church associated with their school.

Similarly, the headteachers are more likely to worship in the church associated with their school than the other members of staff. Thus, 23% of the headteachers worship most Sundays in the parish church associated with their school, compared with 8% of the rest of the teaching staff. Although deputy headteachers, like headteachers, are more likely to attend church services somewhere on a Sunday than other members of staff, they are no more likely than the other members of staff to attend the church associated with their school.

School choice

The teachers whom pupils meet in church schools in a rural diocese are not generally different from the teachers they would meet in neighbouring county schools. The majority of the teachers working in Church of England schools have had experience of teaching in other types of schools before taking up their present post. More than two-thirds (69%) of them have had previous experience teaching in a county school, while 5% have taught in a Roman Catholic school and 8% have taught in the independent sector.

Of the teachers currently employed in controlled schools, 33% had previous experience of a Church of England controlled school, 20% of a Church of England aided school, 6% of a Roman Catholic aided school, 72% of a county school, and 6% of an independent school. Of the teachers currently employed in aided schools, 16% had previous experience of a Church of England aided school, 20% of a Church of England controlled school, 3% of a Roman Catholic aided school, 64% of a county school, and 10% of an independent school. These figures indicate that there is a considerable degree of interchange between the various types of school and that many of the staff currently teaching in Church of England schools are in the position of being able to draw upon their own experience to make considered comparisons between teaching in church schools and in other types of school.

Moreover, the majority of the teachers working in rural church primary schools are not particularly conscious of the distinction between church and county schools. For example, two-thirds of those currently teaching in Church of England schools say that they did not deliberately choose to teach in a church school: 53% say that they have no particular preference as to the kind of school they work in, 13% say that they would actually have preferred to get a job in a county school, 1% would have preferred a Roman Catholic school and another 1% would have preferred an independent school. This means that only 32% of the current teaching staff feel that they would generally prefer to teach in a Church of England school.

The commitment to the voluntary sector increases in line with the promotional ladder. While only 25% of the teachers in scale one, two or three posts say that they actually prefer to work in a church voluntary aided or voluntary controlled school, this proportion increases to 37% of those who hold deputy headships and 47% of those who hold headships.

Those teaching in aided schools have a higher level of commitment to church schools than those teaching in controlled schools: 35% of those teaching in aided schools say that they actually prefer to be in an aided school, while 7% wish that they were in a Church of England controlled school, 9% wish they were in a county school, 1% wish they were in a Roman Catholic aided school, and another 1% wish they were in an independent school. The remaining 48% say that they have no real preference.

By way of comparison, 24% of those teaching in controlled schools say that they actually prefer to be in a controlled school, while 4% wish they were in a Church of England aided school, 14% wish they were in a county school, 1% wish they were in a Roman Catholic aided school and another 1% wish they were in an independent school. The remaining 55% say that they have no real preference.

School policy

The majority of church schools in the diocese are currently operated as neighbourhood schools, functioning in terms of their admission policy in ways very similar to that of their neighbouring county schools. Interestingly, only half (50%) of those currently teaching in these schools consider that this is an appropriate policy for Church of England schools. Just 11% argue that the Church of England should give priority to withdrawing from the system of church schools altogether, while the remaining 39% consider that the Church of England should give priority to providing some special provision specifically for parents who wish their children to have a church education. This means that one in every ten of the teachers working in the rural church school system believes that the system should be totally abandoned, while another four in every ten believe that the system is being employed in the wrong way.

The feeling that Church of England schools should be geared more to making some special provision for those families who want a church education for their children is more pronounced among those teaching in aided schools: 51% of the teachers in aided schools feel that this should be the educational priority of the Church of England, compared with 33% of those in controlled schools. It is, however, those closest to the administrative structure of the present church schools who least favour this notion: only 32% of the headteachers argue in favour of Church of England schools catering for those children whose parents specifically wish for a church education, compared with 41% of those in scale one, two or three posts.

About half (52%) of those currently teaching in the Church of England schools in the diocese feel that the present balance between aided, controlled and county schools is about right. The other half feels that it is time that some changes were made.

Those teaching in aided schools tend to feel that the changes should be made within the controlled sector: 42% of the teachers in aided schools argue that more controlled schools should be encouraged to adopt aided status, while 14% argue that more controlled schools should be encouraged to become county schools. They are much less critical of the present situation regarding the aided schools, with only 13% arguing that more aided schools should be encouraged to adopt controlled status and 10% arguing that more aided schools should become county schools.

On the other hand, those teaching in controlled schools tend to feel that the main changes should be made within the aided sector: 24% of the teachers in controlled schools argue that more aided schools should become controlled, compared with only 13% who argue the other case that more controlled schools should become aided.

This wide range of views about the function and future of the church school system held by those who actually teach in these schools indicates that the present study was indeed timely. The following chapters look in greater depth and detail at these views.

5 ATTITUDES TO CHURCH SCHOOLS

The analysis of the attitudes of those who teach in church schools towards the church school system is a complex undertaking. As chapter three has already discussed, the questionnaire was designed so as to make available detailed information about nine key aspects of the teachers' attitudes to church schools. The nine areas are described in this chapter under the following headings: (1) teachers, (2) admissions policy, (3) future direction, (4) criticisms, (5) commitment, (6) religious education, (7) the diocese, (8) the local church, (9) the clergy. Although these nine headings represent relatively independent areas, there is inevitably some overlap between them. They have been chosen to chart a convenient route through a mass of detailed information about the way in which the teachers feel about church schools. They do not represent, nor are they intended to represent, a description of the factor analytic structure of teachers' attitudes.

This chapter proposes to look at these nine areas in turn and to do so in such a way that we shall learn something about the overall attitudes of the whole group of teachers in the sample and also something about the differences between those who teach in aided and in controlled schools. As a technique of reporting, attention will be drawn to differences between the attitudes of those in aided and controlled schools whenever differences exist to a statistically significant degree. When such differences in attitudes do not exist only the response of the whole group of teachers will be recorded. The detailed statistics on which this chapter is based are presented in tables 5.1 through 5.9.

Teachers

There are many different routes along which teaching staff have been recruited into church schools. There are some teachers who say that they placed religious criteria first. These are the teachers who have made up their minds, for one reason or another, that they want to teach in a church school and they have deliberately set out to find such a post for themselves. There are other teachers who say that they place educational criteria first. These are the teachers who have made up their minds what kind of teaching post they are seeking and they have given little weight to whether the school in which they find this kind of post is of a religious or secular foundation. There are other teachers who have been more influenced by social, geographical or economic considerations.

Given such a wide variety of possible reasons for teaching in a church school in the first place, how committed are the present teaching staff in a rural diocese to being in a church school? Are they there by choice or by accident? All told, only 19% of the teachers say that they applied for their present post specifically because it was in a Church of England school. The proportion is considerably higher in the aided schools (37%) than in the controlled schools (10%). While 19% believe that they were specifically attracted to their present post because it was in a church school, only 6% are so convinced of their preference that they go on to say that they would not have applied for their present post had it been in a county school. Again the proportion is higher in the aided schools (13%) than in the controlled schools (2%).

Having applied for a post in a Church of England school, to what extent do these teachers feel that the school should take the religious question into account in selecting its staff, or look for any special professional qualifications among the applicants? Less than one in four (23%) of the teachers believe that only committed church people should be appointed to teach in Church of England schools. Similarly, less than one in four (22%) believe that teachers should receive any special initial training for work in Church of England schools. Those who teach in aided schools are twice as likely to consider that only committed church people should be appointed to posts in church schools (40%/16%) and to consider that teachers in church schools should receive special initial training (35%/17%).

Now that they are actually teaching in a church school, the teachers are more likely to be critical of their ability to respond adequately to the situation than they were to consider that they needed any special initial training to enter the situation. In particular, two-fifths (40%) of the teachers from both aided and controlled schools feel their schools lack the qualified and effective teachers of religion which they think should be part of a church school. A quarter (25%) of the teachers in controlled schools and two-fifths (42%) of those in aided schools reckon that, having been appointed to a church school, teachers should receive special in-service training to equip them more adequately for their work.

In summary, the majority of teachers in a rural diocese do not wish to assert the distinctiveness of church schools in terms of the teaching staff

71

which they recruit. However, some of them consider that, once recruited, teachers in church schools should undertake special in-service training to equip them to express more adequately the church-related nature of the school.

Admissions policy

Since the 1944 Education Act, Church of England aided schools have operated two different kinds of admission policies. Some aided schools have functioned like county schools, specifically or exclusively to serve the neighbourhood in which they are located. Other aided schools have formulated an admissions policy intended to give varying levels of priority to those who seek a distinctive education on denominational or religious grounds.

Now under the greater parental freedom of choice provided within the 1980 Education Act, aided and controlled schools alike are free to emphasise their peculiar characteristics in the school prospectus in order to attract parents seeking particular educational provisions for their children. To what extent do those who currently teach in church schools believe that these schools should aim at any different kind of pupil intake from county schools? To what extent should Church of England schools market to Anglican parents, or seek to serve those with special needs in any way which is distinctive?

The majority of those who teach in rural church primary schools believe that church schools should operate the same form of admissions policy as county schools and be good neighbourhood schools. Indeed, only about one in seven of the teachers (14%) argue against the idea that church schools should admit every child from the neighbourhood just like county schools. Those who teach in aided schools (33%) are much more likely than those in controlled schools (5%) to argue that the pupil intake of church schools should be different from that of county schools.

Those who argue against church schools being primarily neighbour-hood schools, in the same sense as county schools, generally take the view that they should mainly admit children of church-going parents, of whatever denomination, who wish for a church-related education. This is the position adopted by 6% of the teachers in controlled schools and 32% of those in aided schools. Only a very small minority of the teachers (3% in controlled schools and 13% in aided schools) would take the stronger denominational line and wish to see Church of

England schools operated exclusively for the children of practising Anglicans.

While the majority (88%) of the teachers remain convinced that Church of England schools should admit every child from the neighbourhood just like county schools, half of them (48%) would also want to argue that Anglican parents should be encouraged to send their children to a Church of England school. This is an interesting situation for two reasons.

First, it indicates that half of the teachers (42% in controlled schools and 63% in aided schools) possibly feel that there is something distinctive about Church of England schools from which the children of church members can benefit.

Second, it indicates that these teachers do not generally feel that this denominational distinctiveness needs to militate against the school serving its neighbourhood function in the usual way. What they seem to be suggesting is that Church of England schools can serve an additional function, not an alternative function. While the main job of Church of England schools may well be to cater for the local neighbourhood, they might well also have the additional function of catering for the children of church-going parents from a wider area.

One of the justifications advanced from time to time for the church's continued involvement in the state maintained sector of education is that church schools are able to offer a distinctively caring environment, appropriate perhaps for children with special needs. To what extent would the teachers in church schools wish to argue that, in addition to their neighbourhood function, these schools should also give priority to children with special needs? This view is taken by one in five (21%) of the teachers in controlled schools and by one in three (32%) of the teachers in aided schools.

In summary, the majority of teachers in a rural diocese do not wish to assert the distinctiveness of church schools in terms of denying their service to the local neighbourhood, although many of them would argue that these schools have an additional service to offer to Christian parents.

Future direction

If those who currently teach in church schools were asked to shape the future direction to be taken by church schools, what kind of policy would they wish to encourage? Do they in fact see a future for church schools, and, if so, what would this future look like?

Only a comparatively small minority of the teachers do not envisage a future for church schools in one form or another. Just one in ten argue that the Church of England has too many schools, or suggest that the Church of England should hand over its schools to the state. A much larger proportion are adamant that the Church of England does not have too many schools (51%) and actively resist the notion that church schools should be given over to the state (69%).

Those who wish to dismantle the church school system are not generally prompted by the desire to save church money: only 2% of the teachers argue that the Church of England is putting too much of its money into church schools. Their reasons for wishing to abolish church schools are based on the notion that the system is now inappropriate for today's society: 16% of the teachers in controlled schools and 10% of the teachers in aided schools say that they feel that the church school system has outlived its usefulness.

The majority (66%) of the teachers feel positively that church schools still have a useful role to fulfil in today's society. Moreover, there is considerable interest among the teachers in the ways in which this role can best be fulfilled and expanded. Two ideas in particular attract considerable attention.

Historically Anglican schools were seen as part of the struggle conducted by the various Christian denominations to assert their identity and denominational differences. Now there is much greater concern among the churches to explore co-operation, to practise ecumenism and to seek varying degrees of unity. While the majority of the teachers feel that it is right to preserve the place of church schools in society, they are much less convinced about the appropriateness of preserving the denominational distinctivenesses of these schools: 68% of the teachers say that they would support the development of interdenominational schools, compared with only 10% who would not give their support to this movement. Moreover, most of those who would not support interdenominational schools adopt this view not because they are opposed to ecumenism, but because they are opposed to church schools *per se*.

When thinking about the possibility of ecumenical co-operation, it is necessary to bear in mind that at present, apart from the Church of England, it is only the Roman Catholic church which has a substantial stake in the state maintained sector of education. More than half (52%) of the teachers in Anglican church schools feel that they know insufficient about the Roman Catholic church schools in the area to be able to draw comparisons between the two systems. 23% feel that the

Roman Catholic church makes a better job of running its church schools than the Church of England, while the other 25% feel that the Church of England is doing the better job of the two. There seems to be a need for greater interchange between teachers from these two denominations so that they can become better informed about each other.

The present balance of church schools in the diocese is very heavily weighted towards provision for the younger child; 60% of those who currently teach in church aided first, primary or middle schools feel that the balance should be re-distributed by developing more church secondary, middle or upper schools. They consider that the present situation is deficient in the sense that many of the children educated in church aided schools to the age of nine, eleven or even thirteen are then unable to complete their secondary education in a church-related school. This view is also shared by a third (33%) of those who teach in church controlled first, primary or middle schools in the diocese.

In summary the majority of teachers in a rural diocese not only wish the distinctive contribution of church schools to remain, but for this to be developed in terms of more secondary schools and greater ecumenical co-operation.

Criticisms

As chapter one has already indicated, church schools are certainly not without their critics in the 1980s. Questions are raised about the appropriateness of church schools both from secular voices outside the churches and from some groups within the churches. To what extent are the teachers currently working in church schools critical of these schools either in terms of their effects on the children who attend them, or in terms of their effects on society at large?

From within the church it is sometimes said that the church schools do more harm than good by alienating their pupils from religion. The majority of those who actually teach in rural church primary schools strongly reject this idea. Only a little over one in every ten of the teachers agrees that this is true: 12% believe that church schools often alienate their pupils from the church, and 11% believe that church schools often help to turn pupils away from Christianity itself. On the other hand, six in every ten of the teachers firmly reject these accusations, while the remaining three in every ten keep a relatively open mind on the issue.

Other voices, both within the church and outside, argue that church schools are socially or racially divisive. This objection to church schools argues that they favour white middle class values, and give unfair privileges to some children. Again the teachers who actually teach in the church schools in this rural diocese seem to find little evidence to support these notions. Just 7% agree with the idea that church schools are socially divisive. Similarly, just 7% agree with the idea that church schools are racially divisive. A much larger body of teachers in the diocese deny that church schools are either socially (75%) or racially (70%) divisive in their own experience. The teachers emphasise that the criticisms voiced against church schools from an urban background cannot necessarily be generalised to the rural situation.

The idea that church schools give unfair advantages to some children is even more strongly rejected by the teachers: 82% clearly reject this idea compared with just 5% who support it. The remaining 13% say that they are not sure about the matter.

While only 5% of the teachers go along with the idea that church schools confer unfair privileges on some of the pupils, a larger proportion (17%) feel that church schools give unfair advantages to Christian teachers in the promotion stakes. For example, they seem to believe that it is easier to get a headship in a church school if you happen to be an Anglican, and they think that this is unfair to the teaching profession as a whole. However, this remains a minority view, clearly rejected by 47% of those currently teaching in church schools and left as an open issue by the remaining 36% of them.

In summary, the majority of teachers do not see church schools in a rural diocese to be distinctive in the negative sense of being harmful to the children who attend them, to the teaching profession itself or to society at large.

Commitment

When church schools were being founded in the nineteenth century, the trust deeds often specified that one of the functions of the school was to teach the doctrine of the Church of England. In this context, communication of the Christian faith, or catechesis, was firmly seen as an aspect of general education: church schools were to be communities in which the faith was taught and in which denominational worship had a proper place. It was assumed that these activities would be conducted by teachers who themselves were committed to the Christian faith.

Under the 1944 Education Act, both aided and controlled schools retained the right to provide denominational worship for the whole school, subject to a conscience clause. Aided schools retained the right to provide denominational instruction, from which individual children could be withdrawn by their parents' request, while controlled schools retained the right to provide denominational instruction for those children whose parents specifically requested it. In the 1950s, even the agreed syllabus teaching in county schools and controlled schools was strongly Christian in character and implicitly or explicitly assumed the Christian commitment of those who were teaching it.

During the 1960s and 1970s the whole question of the place of religious commitment in education came under severe scrutiny. Educational theorists have been arguing the case that catechesis and education are contradictory categories, that worship should have no place in a state maintained school, and that religious education should neither proceed from the teacher's own commitment nor aim at achieving the child's commitment. How far has this kind of theory influenced the views of those who teach in church primary schools in a rural diocese?

To begin with, two-thirds (65%) of the teachers in church schools have accepted the notion that it is not the task of county schools to initiate children into a religious faith. A further 11% have not made up their minds on this issue, and 24% still think it is appropriate for county schools to set out to do this. At the same time, half (51%) of the teachers have transferred this notion to church schools as well, and they argue that it is not the task of Church of England schools to initiate children into a religious faith. Again, just 11% have not made up their minds on this issue, leaving 38% who still think it is appropriate for Church of England schools to set out to do this. On this issue there is a clear distinction of opinion between those who teach in aided and controlled schools. While only 30% of the teachers in controlled schools think it is right for church schools to initiate children into a religious faith, the proportion rises to 55% of the teachers in aided schools.

Precisely what the teachers have in mind when they say that it is not the task of church schools to initiate children into a religious faith is grasped by analysing the kinds of religious objectives they accept for church schools and the kinds they reject. While the majority view is clearly against trying to convert children to the Christian faith, it is not against teaching the Christian faith, conducting Christian worship and even mixing education and evangelism.

Thus, although 58% of the teachers are quite adamant that it is educationally unsound for Church of England schools to try to convert children to the Christian faith, only 11% argue that it is educationally unsound for Church of England schools to try to teach the Christian faith. Moreover, only 11% are in favour of abandoning the idea of worship from school assembly, while 46% feel that it is appropriate to mix education with some evangelism.

The consensus of the teachers within church schools in the diocese is that it is not inappropriate to allow the Christian faith to influence their view of education. Paul Hirst, the Professor of Education in Cambridge, has been arguing for more than a decade that it is a philosophical nonsense to speak of a specifically Christian view of education. While 30% of the teachers in church schools agree with Hirst's conclusion, another 58% clearly reject it.

In summary, the majority of teachers in a rural diocese are willing to see the distinctiveness of church schools to include some commitment to the Christian faith and the involvement of pupils in Christian worship, but only as long as this does not imply any form of aggressive indoctrination or the violation of the child's ultimate freedom to make up his or her own mind.

Religious education

The use made of the religious education component within the school curriculum is one of the most obvious areas to examine closely for the possible distinctiveness of church schools. To what extent do the teachers in church schools believe that their religious education should in some senses be different from that in county schools? The views of those teaching in controlled and aided schools differ greatly on this question: 66% of the teachers in controlled schools argue that the aims of religious education in Church of England schools should be the same as those in county schools. By way of comparison, only 39% of the teachers in aided schools hold this view.

In what ways, then, is it thought that religious education in church schools should differ from religious education in county schools? The truth of the matter is that the majority of the teachers in church schools are rather muddled in their thinking about religious education. They find themselves repeating some of the clichés of current educational theory, but failing to recognise the incompatibility of some of the views they profess to hold. For example, educational theory of the 1970s clearly moved the aim of religious education from promoting the pupils' commitment to developing their understanding. Jean Holm, senior lecturer in religious education, Homerton College, Cambridge, did much to popularise the notion that "religious education should help children to understand what religion is and what it would mean to take a religion seriously". Nine out of ten teachers in church schools (89% in controlled and 92% in aided) have accepted this phrase and say that they agree with it. The implication of this objective is that religious education should not be confessional in the sense of pressing for the pupils' commitment to any particular religious standpoint. While accepting the phraseology of Jean Holm's aim, 66% of the teachers in controlled schools and 88% in aided schools concurrently agree with the very different aim that Church of England schools should encourage their pupils to accept and to practise the Christian faith.

While the majority of the teachers accept the place of confessional religious education in the rural church primary school, they are much less likely to support the idea of specifically denominational religious education. Thus less than one in five of the teachers (13% in controlled schools and 29% in aided schools) argue that good religious education should include denominational teaching. Similarly only 6% of the teachers in controlled schools and 23% in aided schools see a proper place for the celebration of communion in the church school. A much higher proportion of the teachers, however, wish to see their pupils taught about the communion service. This is the view held by one-third (35%) of teachers in controlled schools and by two-thirds (66%) of teachers in aided schools.

A lot has been said in recent years about the importance of the home and the church in the task of Christian education. How do the teachers in church schools feel about this in relationship to the role of their schools? The majority (88%) of the teachers in church schools have accepted the theory that the home is more important than the school in determining the child's religious commitment. They have not, however, generally gone on to assert that schools should not be implicated in the job of Christian education. Only 20% of the teachers in controlled schools and 10% in aided schools agree with the idea that Christian education is the job of parents and the church, but not of the school.

In summary, the majority of teachers in a rural diocese are uncertain both as to how distinctive religious education should be in church schools, and to the nature of this distinctiveness should it be asserted.

Diocese

Historically church schools were founded as independent and autonomous trusts and there is still comparatively little centralised control within the Anglican system of church schools. Currently the diocese offers a range of advisory and support facilities for church schools through the diocesan education committee and through the full-time and part-time staff members with the diocesan education team. For example, the schools officer is available for consultation on matters relating to buildings, finance, governors and relationships with the local education authority. The diocesan religious education adviser is available to offer support on matters of curriculum, resources, syllabuses and so on. To what extent do teachers in rural church primary schools look to the diocese for advice and support? Do they feel that the diocese offers enough support? Do the schools themselves seem reluctant to accept help when it is offered?

Four-fifths of the teachers seem quite clear that the days of independence and autonomy should be over for church schools. They seem to feel that the individual schools have much to gain from contact with the diocese, and this is especially the case among teachers in aided schools. Thus, 92% of the teachers in aided schools and 72% of those in controlled schools believe that the diocese should take the initiative in fostering links between Church of England schools and local churches.

At the same time, there is quite a feeling that the diocese is not doing enough at present to promote links with individual schools. The biggest complaint against the diocese is that Church of England schools generally lack good and appropriate materials for religious education: 61% of the teachers in aided schools and 58% of those in controlled schools argue that Church of England schools need better teaching materials for religious education than are presently available. Related to this problem of resources for religious education, 38% of the teachers in aided schools and 36% of those in controlled schools feel that the diocese could be giving a lot more help to those who teach religious education in church schools.

On a wider front, a third (33%) of the teachers in aided schools and a quarter (26%) of the teachers in controlled schools feel that the Church of England just does not take enough interest in its church schools. There are ways in which these teachers tend to feel isolated or betrayed by the church responsible for the school. A quarter of the teachers place the blame for the neglect they experience firmly at the feet of their diocesan education office: 24% of the teachers in aided schools and 27% of those in controlled schools say that their own school does not have enough contact with the diocesan education office.

Looking for the reasons for this feeling of insufficient support from the diocese, the teachers tend to believe that the fault must lie with the central administration and not with the individual schools. Only 8% of the teachers suggest that the local schools themselves are reluctant to accept help from the diocese in such matters as the teaching of religious education.

In summary, the majority of teachers in a rural diocese feel that the distinctiveness of church schools should include a greater degree of contact with and support from the diocesan education office. A number of teachers feel that the present level of support offered by the diocese is inadequate.

Local church

The amount of contact between the local church and the church school situated in its parish varies greatly from place to place. Some schools have more contact with their local church than they would really wish, while others wish that the local church would take a greater interest in the school. How do the teachers themselves feel about this issue?

More teachers feel that the local church does not take enough interest in their school than those who think that it does. In the controlled schools, 31% of the teachers complain that the local church does not take enough interest, while 26% feel that it does take enough interest and the remaining 43% do not really care one way or the other. In the aided schools, 48% complain that the local church does not take enough interest, compared with only 22% who feel that it does take enough interest and 30% who do not really care one way or the other.

In what ways do these teachers feel that the local church should show more interest? The three areas to which they point are through the local church building itself, through the clergy and through the school governors appointed by the church. Of these three ways, it is the governors who are most severely criticised by the teaching staff.

Just 16% of the teachers in controlled schools and 20% of those in aided schools are dissatisfied with the level of contact between their school and the local church building. This proportion rises to 17% of teachers in controlled schools and 26% of the teachers in aided schools who are dissatisfied with the level of contact between their school and the local clergy. By way of comparison, 49% of the teachers in controlled schools and 64% of the teachers in aided schools are dissatisfied with the level of contact between their school and the governors appointed by the local church.

Under the 1944 Education Act, which was still the controlling act at the time when the survey was conducted, the church is responsible for appointing two-thirds of the governors to aided schools and one-third of the governors to controlled schools. While the precise proportions change under the 1980 Education Act, it remains the case that the church is responsible for appointing the majority of the governors to aided schools and a minority of the governors to controlled schools. These are known as 'foundation governors'. The foundation governors have a special responsibility for seeing that the intentions of the original trust deed by which the school was founded are carried out in accordance with the legal provision of the statutory education acts. The fact that half of the teachers in controlled schools and two-thirds of those in aided schools are critical of the lack of support they receive from the foundation governors is a serious indictment on the way in which representatives of the church are appointed to such a post of responsibility and on the way in which they are inadequately trained for that responsibility.

Looked at another way, less than one in four (23%) of the teachers from both aided and controlled schools feel that the foundation governors take an active part in the life of the school. Possibly many are glad that the foundation governors do not take a more active role, because there is quite a feeling that the foundation governors do not really understand their job anyway. Thus, 41% of the teachers in aided schools and 32% of those in controlled schools lament that the foundation governors do not adequately understand the role of Church of England schools in today's society.

In summary, one of the major distinctive features of church schools is the way in which foundation governors are appointed by the church and are able to foster links between the school and the church. The majority of teachers in a rural diocese feel that these foundation governors give inadequate support and help to the school.

Clergy

The Anglican clergy have been, and often still are, the major link between the church school and the church. Generally the parish priest finds himself in the position of being an ex officio foundation governor of the school, and quite often the governors assume that he is the ex officio chairman as well, even when this is not strictly the case. In situations when the school serves multiple parishes under the care of more than one clergyman, the foundation governors can sometimes be found to include more than one clergyman.

As well as serving as foundation governors, the clergy associated with church schools often come into contact with their church school by making informal pastoral visits, taking assemblies or taking the distinctive denominationally based religious education classes. From a slightly earlier survey conducted among the parochial clergy of the same rural diocese, it emerged that 94% of the clergy with aided schools and 81% of those with controlled make informal visits to their schools at least occasionally, while 78% of those with aided schools and 41% of those with controlled schools do so at least weekly.

Four-fifths (81%) of the clergy who have controlled schools in their parishes take assemblies occasionally, while 36% do so weekly. A slightly higher proportion (89%) of the clergy who have aided schools in their parishes take assemblies occasionally, while 39% do so weekly. Nearly three-fifths (56%) of the clergy with controlled schools take religious education lessons occasionally, while 34% do so weekly. A much higher proportion (83%) of the clergy with aided schools take religious education lessons occasionally, while 44% do so weekly.

Given the fact that so many of the clergy who have the opportunity of contact with the church school in their parish actually make use of that opportunity, what are the feelings of the teaching staff about the way in which clergy relate to church schools?

We have already seen from the previous section that there is a considerable degree of dissatisfaction with the foundation governors. In general, however, the teachers do not seem to feel that the clergy are any worse than the other foundation governors, and many of the clergy may well be an improvement on some of the others. Thus, 39% of the teachers feel that the clergy make good governors, compared with only 14% who say that they are not good governors. The really significant feature, however, is that the other 47% of the teachers are not really sure. Possibly they are not content with the support the school receives from the clergy as foundation governors, but they cannot envisage the local church nominating more adequate foundation governors in the place of the clergy.

There is quite a feeling among the teachers that church schools are neglected by the clergy. This is especially so in the case of aided schools, where 57% of the teachers say that the clergy do not take enough interest in church schools. In the case of controlled schools, 33% of the teachers feel that the clergy do not take enough interest in church schools, and the majority of the others do not wish the clergy to take an interest in the school anyway.

A small minority of the teachers have adopted a strong stance against all involvement of the clergy in the local school: 12% of the teachers in aided schools and 15% of those in controlled schools say that by coming into school clergy often do more harm than good. A much greater number are happy with the clergy coming into schools, but have reservations about the competence of the clergy to make good educational use of their time once they are in the school. While the majority are happy for the clergy to visit, fewer are happy when the clergy conduct assemblies and fewer still are happy when they take lessons. Thus, 26% of the teachers say that the clergy are not competent to lead assemblies, and 38% say that the clergy are not competent to teach or to take lessons in church schools. The majority feel that, if the clergy must take lessons, then they should follow a clear syllabus and be given as many guidelines and as much help as possible.

The majority of the teachers feel that the main problem is that the clergy are not generally aware of current educational thinking. In fact, only 18% of the teachers feel that the clergy are sufficiently up to date on current educational thinking to be able to make a good contribution to the educational life of the school. As the majority of the teachers understand the situation, the problem goes back to one of basic training: 61% of the teachers say that in their experience the clergy do not seem to be adequately trained for involvement in Church of England schools. By way of comparison, only 10% of the teachers feel that the clergy have been adequately trained for this kind of job, while the remaining 29% say that they do not know enough about the situation to be able to come to a reasonable view on the matter.

In summary, the majority of teachers in a rural diocese are happy for the distinctive role of church schools to include contact with the local clergy, but they are convinced that, if this role is to persist, the clergy need to be adequately trained in order to be able to fulfill this aspect of their work more satisfactorily.

6 ATTITUDES TO TEACHING

The purpose of this chapter is to analyse the attitudes of those who teach in church schools towards their work as teachers. What are these teachers setting out to do during their time in the classroom? What do they regard as their personal educational priorities and as the educational goals of their schools?

The views of teachers in church schools on these kinds of issues may well be the same as those of teachers in county schools. The purpose of the present chapter is to describe the views of those who teach in church schools, rather than to ascertain the extent to which their views reflect the peculiar ethos or goals of church schools. After this chapter has described the attitudes of those who teach in church schools, the next chapter will go on to analyse the extent to which the teachers regard their views as being influenced specifically by the fact that they teach in a church school. In other words, the present chapter proposes to describe the educational *characteristics* of Church of England primary schools in a rural diocese, while the next chapter will look at the educational *distinctiveness* of these church schools.

In order to provide a thorough description of the teachers' perceptions of both the educational characteristics and the educational distinctiveness of church schools, the questionnaire included items about eight key aspects of school life. These eight areas are described as (1) the curriculum, (2) religious education, (3) the Christian community, (4) school ethos, (5) the relationship between the school and the local community, (6) the contribution of the school to the moral development of their pupils, (7) traditional educational methods and (8) progressive educational methods.

Once again, in this chapter attention will be drawn to differences between the attitudes of those in aided and controlled schools whenever differences exist to a statistically significant degree. When such differences in attitude do not exist, only the response of the whole group of teachers will be reported. The detailed statistics on which this chapter is based are presented in tables 6.1 through 6.8.

Curriculum

There is a wide range of subjects which parents are likely to expect to find taught in all primary schools. These may well include subject areas like (in alphabetical order) art, english, environmental studies, maths, moral education, music, physical education, reading, religious education, science, sex education and social studies. How do the teachers themselves rate the relative importance of these subject areas?

When the importance of the twelve subject areas listed above is rated by the teachers on a five point scale, a clear rank ordering of priorities emerges. At the top of the list of priorities come the three Rs: maths, english and reading all vie for the top place, being rated as 'very important' by between 93% and 96% of the teachers. Moral education takes fourth place, being regarded as 'very important' by 77% of the teachers, and as 'quite important' by another 20%. Then in descending order of importance come science, environmental studies, art and music. This leaves religious education in ninth place, being rated as 'very important' by 47% of the teachers and as 'quite important' by a further 47%. Very close behind religious education come physical education and social studies. Lagging much further behind in twelfth place comes sex education. Sex education is regarded as 'very important' by just 12% of the teachers and as 'quite important' by a further 37%. One in four (24%) of the teachers in fact argue that sex education is not an appropriate aim in a church school.

There are very few significant differences between the curriculum priorities of those who teach in controlled schools and those who teach in aided schools. The only two areas in which differences do occur are in relationship to religious education and sex education. As far as religious education is concerned, those who teach in aided schools accord this area a higher priority: 98% of aided school teachers rate religious education as one of their important educational goals, compared with 91% of controlled school teachers. As far as sex education is concerned, those who teach in aided schools accord this area a lower priority: 44% of aided school teachers rate sex education as one of their important goals, compared with 50% of controlled school teachers. The importance attributed to religious education and sex education are, thus, inversely related. Interestingly, the differences found in these two areas of religious education and sex education are not reflected at all in the wider area of moral education.

Another way of emphasising the relative importance given to religious education in controlled and aided schools is by recalculating the rank order in which the teachers place the twelve curriculum areas for aided and controlled schools separately. According to this recalculation, religious education occupies fifth place in the aided school, coming immediately after maths, english, reading and science, and tenth place in the controlled school, coming only above sex education and social studies.

In summary, the curriculum priorities of teachers in aided and controlled schools in a rural diocese are identical, except in relationship to religious education and sex education. In both types of school a great emphasis is placed on the traditional values of the three Rs.

Religious education

Having examined in the previous section how the priority given to religious education relates to the priority given to other school subjects in church primary schools in a rural diocese, we turn now to a closer inspection of what the teachers mean by religious education. To what extent do they consider that their school should be teaching Christianity to the pupils, or should they concentrate also on teaching about world religions? What priority should church schools give to teaching about Jesus, the bible, the church, church services and so on? Do teachers prefer to keep religious education as a distinct component on the timetable, or do they prefer to integrate it with secular studies?

The majority of the teachers are very clear that their priority is towards teaching Christianity, rather than teaching world religions. Thus, 52% rate teaching about Christianity as very important, compared with 19% who rate teaching about world religions as very important. Looked at from another perspective, only 2% of the teachers do not regard teaching about Christianity as an appropriate goal for church schools and just 7% regard it as an acceptable but unimportant goal. By way of comparison, 9% of the teachers do not regard teaching about world religions as an appropriate goal for church schools, and a further 18% regard it as an acceptable but unimportant goal.

Teaching about Christianity to children might well include components about Jesus, the bible, the church and church services. Teachers in church schools are quite clear about the different levels of priority they ascribe to such components. They set teaching about God and Jesus firmly in the first place: between 56% and 58% believe that it is very important to teach about Jesus and about God. In second place, they set teaching about the bible: 37% believe that it is very important to teach about the bible. Then in third place, they set teaching about the church: 22% believe that it is very important to teach about the church. Finally, in fourth place they set teaching about church services: 9% believe that it is very important to teach about church services.

Four out of five (81%) of the teachers believe that it is important to integrate religious education and secular studies. Only a small minority (6%) believe that it is totally inappropriate to integrate religious education in this way, while the remaining 13% accept integration in principle but do not attach a great deal of importance to the notion.

While teachers in aided schools and in controlled schools both attach the same level of importance to teaching about world religions, the teachers in aided schools tend to attach an even greater importance to teaching about Christianity. Thus, 95% of the aided school teachers believe that it is important to teach about Christianity, compared with 88% of the controlled school teachers.

This difference is also reflected in the weight given by the teachers to the various components of a Christian curriculum. It is most clearly reflected in the weight given to teaching about church services. Thus, 95% of the aided school teachers believe that it is important to teach about Jesus, compared with 87% of the controlled school teachers; 93% of the aided school teachers believe that it is important to teach about the bible, compared with 84% of the controlled school teachers; 87% of the aided school teachers believe that it is important to teach about the church, compared with 72% of the controlled school teachers; 74% of the aided school teachers believe that it is important to teach about church services, compared with 44% of the controlled school teachers.

The other significant difference between the views of those who teach in aided and controlled schools concerns the integration of religious education and secular subjects. The aided school teachers (89%) are more likely to emphasise the importance of the integration of religious education than the controlled school teachers (77%).

In summary, teachers in church primary schools in a rural diocese give a higher priority to teaching Christianity than to teaching world religions, but the kind of Christian education which they envisage as appropriate within church schools is that which places a higher priority on introducing children to religious ideas than to religious practices.

Christian community

When church schools were being founded in the nineteenth century, there was a clear idea that these were places where Christian community was to be established. The 1944 Education Act also presupposed such an environment for county schools, where worship was to take place daily and where religious education was to be based on agreed syllabus non-denominational Christian teaching. To what extent do teachers in church schools today feel that their school should be an extension of the Christian community, a place where Christian values are put into practice, where religion is taught by committed Christians, and where a Christian assembly takes place on a regular basis, or even daily?

Just as the teachers' understanding of Christian education gave priority to the more general principles of Christianity rather than to the practice of Christianity, so their concept of a Christian community concentrates on the more general principles. This means that 76% of the teachers consider that putting Christian values into practice should be a very important goal of their school. The slightly more specific notion of providing an atmosphere of Christian community is regarded as very important by 56%. The more specific notion of providing a regular Christian assembly is regarded as very important by 47%. Then the really specific notions of saying classroom prayers, having a regular communion service celebrated in school, and preparing pupils for confirmation are regarded as very important by 18%, 3% and 2% of the teachers respectively.

Interestingly, the teachers place a much higher value on the school putting into practice Christian values than on employing Christian staff. While 76% believe that it should be a very important goal of their school to put Christian values into practice, only 28% believe that it is very important to have committed Christians on the staff, while about the same proportion (31%) believe that it is very important to have religious education taught by committed Christians. The implication is plainly that, in the view of the teachers, the practice of Christian values is no longer closely bound up with the practice of the Christian religion itself. The school can continue to put Christian values into practice without the need to attract committed Christians to the staff.

While the teachers in controlled and aided schools both place a high emphasis on putting Christian values into practice in their schools, the teachers in aided schools place a significantly higher value on the more specific practices of the Christian community: 96% of the teachers in aided schools believe that one of their goals should be to provide an atmosphere of Christian community, compared with 86% of the teachers in controlled schools; 88% of those in aided schools believe this atmosphere of Christian community should include a daily Christian assembly, compared with 76% of those in controlled schools; 74% of those in aided schools believe that classroom prayers should be said, compared with 48% of those in controlled schools.

Similarly, those who work in aided schools place a higher importance on having committed Christians on the staff. Thus, 73% of the aided school teachers believe that it is an important goal of their school to have committed Christians on the staff, compared with 55% of the controlled school teachers; 79% of the aided school teachers believe that religious education should be taught by committed Christians, compared with 65% of the controlled school teachers.

Those who teach in aided schools are also more inclined to emphasise the appropriateness of the church school embracing distinctively denominational signs of the Christian community. For example, 22% of those who teach in aided schools believe that it is important to have a regular communion service for the school, compared with 6% of those who teach in controlled schools; 27% of those who teach in aided schools believe that it is important for church schools to prepare pupils for confirmation, compared with 10% of those who teach in controlled schools. Looked at from another perspective, 43% of aided school teachers and 59% of controlled school teachers argue that it is educationally inappropriate to have a regular communion service celebrated for the school, while 40% of aided school teachers and 60% of controlled school teachers argue that it is educationally inappropriate for church schools to prepare pupils for confirmation.

In summary, the teachers in church schools in a rural diocese tend to believe that the idea of promoting a Christian community within the school is an important and educationally appropriate principle. The kind of Christian community which they envisage, however, is one which emphasises the importance of Christian values, but does not emphasise the importance of the religious practices underpinning those values.

School ethos

Having reviewed the teachers' views on the curriculum, religious education in particular and the idea of the school as a Christian community, we turn now to an analysis of their views on the overall aims of the hidden curriculum, or what might be called the intention of the school ethos. For example, do they reckon that the main emphasis of the school should be on promoting academic excellence or pupil happiness?

Overall, the goal which the teachers rated most highly was that of creating a caring environment. This was seen to be very important by 95% of the teachers and as quite important by an additional 4%. The teachers understand the creation of such a caring environment to involve, in the following order, respecting each pupil irrespective of ability or appearance, helping the slower pupils, promoting the enjoyment of school, bringing the best out of bright pupils, promoting the pupils' confidence in the staff, and being available to counsel individual children. For example, 91% of the teachers argue that it is a very important goal of the school to respect each pupil irrespective of ability or appearance; 79% argue that it is a very important goal to promote the pupil's confidence in the staff; and 71% believe it is very important to be available to counsel individual children.

The teachers place the promotion of a high level of academic attainment well below all these other priorities. Thus, while 89% regard helping the slower pupils to be very important and 82% regard bringing the best out of bright pupils to be very important, the proportion falls to 54% who believe that it is very important to promote a high level of academic attainment.

There are no significant differences in this section on school ethos between the views of teachers in aided schools and in controlled schools.

In summary, the teachers in church schools in a rural diocese place a much higher value on their schools creating a caring environment than on promoting a high level of academic attainment.

Local community

Although school is an important aspect of a child's life, it is only one aspect among many others. The child is also part of a family and part of a wider community. To what extent do the teachers in church schools feel that the school should develop close contacts with the parents and with other people from the local community? How much responsibility do they feel that the school has to know about the pupils' home backgrounds, and to offer advice and help to their parents when they seek it? As church schools, how importantly do they rate developing links with the local clergy?

Most of the teachers reckon that it is important for the school to develop close links with the pupils' homes. Thus, 81% regard developing close contacts with parents as very important and a further 18% regard this as quite important; 67% think that it is very important to know about the pupils' home backgrounds, while a further 28% regard this as quite important.

Quite a number of parents value the opportunity to talk with their child's teacher about problems they experience with the child at home. Such interviews can run over into the discussion of more personal matters, like marital and financial problems. For some parents the teacher may well be the only professional person whom they feel they know well enough to approach with personal problems. The vast majority of the teachers in church schools agree that it is part of their function to help parents in a variety of ways. Thus, 58% of the teachers regard as very important being available to counsel individual parents, while a further 38% regard it as quite important. In fact, only 1% of the teachers argue that counselling individual parents is an inappropriate demand on their time.

While teachers are keen to develop close contacts with parents, they are much less eager to encourage parents to help in the school itself. Thus, less than a third (31%) of the teachers give a high priority to encouraging parents to help in the school. While the majority of the other teachers do not give this a high priority, very few of them (3%) would want to exclude parents from helping in the school altogether.

The majority of the teachers also consider it important to develop close contact between the school and the local community of which the school is part. Thus, 60% rate such contacts as very important and a further 37% rate them as quite important, leaving only 3% who do not consider such contacts to be important.

While teachers are keen to develop contacts with the local community as a whole, they are less eager to encourage close contacts with the clergy: 64% of the teachers rate developing close contacts with the clergy to be an important goal for their school, compared with 97% who rate developing close contacts with the local community to be important, while 6% regard such an objective to be totally inappropriate for their church school.

The teachers in aided and controlled schools give exactly the same levels of priority to fostering contacts with parents and with the wider local community. Where they do differ, however, is in relationship to developing contacts with the clergy. Those who teach in aided schools give a higher priority to contact with the clergy: 78% of the teachers in aided schools believe that their school should be developing contacts with the clergy, compared with 64% of the teachers in controlled schools. Similarly, 83% of aided school teachers believe that their school should encourage frequent visits from the clergy, compared with 70% of controlled school teachers. While arguing that they should encourage this kind of contact with the local clergy, even the aided school teachers do not place this objective high on their list of priorities. They tend to regard it as quite important, rather than as very important.

In summary, the teachers in church schools in a rural diocese place a high level of importance on developing links with the parents of the pupils who attend the school, and with the wider local community. They do not, however, generally see the local clergy as playing an important part in the set of relationships between the child, the parents and the wider local community.

Images of the moral life

This section turns attention to the views which the teachers hold about the contribution of the school to the moral development of their pupils. What moral values do they regard most highly and how do they see the role of the school in promoting these values?

At the top of their list of moral priorities they place the twin concepts of training the children to think for themselves and teaching them to be honest and truthful: 92% rate teaching children to be honest and truthful as very important, while 91% rate training children to think for themselves as very important. The priority of these teachers is not so much to teach their pupils to obey rules, but rather to help them to make honest and truthful decisions for themselves.

The teachers are much more concerned with promoting self-discipline and the respect and acceptance of others than with instilling traditional moral values, like good manners, obedience, hard work and tidiness. Teaching children good manners is regarded as very important by 67%, obedience as very important by 61%, hard work as very important by 59% and tidiness as very important by 34%. Very few of the teachers suggest that these traditional values should be disregarded, but they would prefer not to place them too close to the top of list of priorities. By way of comparison, 87% of the teachers rate teaching children to accept others as very important, while 85% rate training children in self-discipline as very important.

A third of the teachers are quite clear that the moral education offered by church schools should not include an emphasis on church attendance: 32% argue that it is not an appropriate goal of church schools to train children to go to church regularly. A further 62% accept this as an appropriate goal, but place it low on their list of objectives, leaving only 6% of the teachers who want to argue that training children to go to church regularly should be a very important goal for church schools.

The images of the moral life held by teachers in the aided schools are very close to those held by teachers in the controlled schools in every respect except for that concerned with church attendance. Those who teach in aided schools (47%) are twice as likely to regard training children to go to church regularly as an important goal for church schools as those who teach in controlled schools (24%).

In summary, the teachers in church primary schools in a rural diocese place a much higher value on preparing their pupils to think for themselves and to develop their own moral responsibility than upon training them to obey rules and to attend church. The emphasis is on promoting moral autonomy rather than heteronomy.

Traditional methods

Educational research concerned with the differentiation between traditional and progressive educational methods has identified a range of factors which tend to characterise the traditional approach to education. These include ideas like streaming according to ability, following a regular timetable, giving regular spelling tests or maths tests, and awarding stars or other credits for good work. To what extent do teachers in church schools continue to value such traditional educational methods?

To begin with, streaming according to ability remains very out of fashion. Less than a third (31%) of the teachers believe that streaming is a good thing. Regular timetables for different lessons are more in favour than streaming: 53% of the teachers are in favour of following a regular timetable. The use of regular tests, especially for spelling, continue to find approval among between a half and two-thirds of the teachers: 49% favour giving regular maths tests and 69% favour giving regular spelling tests. More than half of the teachers (56%) value giving stars or other credits for good work. More than three-quarters believe in correcting most spelling and grammatical errors (77%) and in teaching children to know their multiplication tables by heart (76%). Almost all of them (96%) believe in the importance of teaching children to develop clear handwriting.

Firm discipline is given approval by 92% of the teachers, and 68% would go so far as to approve the concept of *strict* discipline. Similarly, 80% expect their pupils to seek permission before leaving the classroom and 79% believe in punishing children for persistent disruptive behaviour.

Those who teach in aided schools tend to be slightly more traditional in their approach than those who teach in controlled schools. This is seen in a variety of ways. For example, 75% of the aided school teachers believe in adopting strict discipline, compared with 65% of the controlled school teachers; 84% of the aided school teachers believe in punishing children for persistent disruptive behaviour, compared with 77% of the controlled school teachers. Regular maths tests are favoured by 59% of those who teach in aided schools, compared with 45% of those who teach in controlled schools. Giving stars or other credits for good work is favoured by 59% of those who teach in aided schools, compared with 54% of those who teach in controlled schools.

This trend for those who teach in aided schools to be more favourably disposed than those who teach in controlled schools to the traditional educational methods is also reflected in their attitude towards streaming: 38% of the aided school teachers support the idea of streaming according to ability, compared with 28% of those who teach in controlled schools.

In summary, while rejecting the traditional educational method of streaming according to ability, the majority of teachers in a rural diocese favour many of the other traditional methods of education. Those who teach in aided schools tend to be slightly more in favour of traditional methods than those who teach in controlled schools.

Progressive methods

In contrast to the traditional approach to education, the features which are thought by educational researchers to characterise the progressive method include adopting an integrated day, following a project approach to learning, encouraging free expression, allowing the children to move around the classroom, allowing the children to decide where they are going to sit, and so on. Having shown in the previous section that the teachers in church schools tend to continue to give approval to many of the traditional educational methods, we turn now to examine the extent to which the corollary might hold good regarding the rejection of progressive methods.

Although the majority of the teachers say that they wish to advocate firm discipline, this does not imply for them a rigid or inflexible approach to education. Alongside firm discipline, the majority of them also value self-expression: 62% say that they rate encouraging self-expression as very important and a further 34% rate it as quite important. Similarly, 83% of the teachers are quite content to allow the children to talk to one another in class, while two-thirds (64%) generally allow the children to move around the classroom. On the other hand, only a quarter (28%) are prepared to allow the children to choose where they sit. The point these teachers want to make is that they give approval to progressive methods so long as the freedom which these methods gives to the children is understood by them to be within firm and fixed boundaries.

The progressive notion of the integrated day receives less support from the teachers than the traditional notion of the regular timetabled periods for different subjects. While 53% of the teachers are in favour of following a regular timetable, only 38% are in favour of adopting an integrated day. Again, the point which a number of the teachers want to make is that the structure of a timetable does not have to militate against flexible and progressive teaching techniques. Two-thirds (67%) of the teachers are very clearly in favour of promoting a, project approach to learning.

Just as the teachers in aided schools are more inclined to favour some of the more traditional educational methods, so they are less inclined to favour some of the progressive educational methods. This is seen most clearly in relationship to their views on project learning and to allowing children to decide where to sit. Thus, 62% of aided school teachers favoured following the project approach to learning, compared with 70% of controlled school teachers; 22% of aided school teachers believe in generally allowing children to decide where to sit, compared with 31% of controlled school teachers.

In summary, although the teachers in church schools in a rural diocese favour many of the traditional goals of education, this does not mean that they also reject all of the more progressive theory. Their approach seems to be to integrate many of the progressive ideas within the framework of a comparatively traditional philosophy.

7 IDEAS OF DISTINCTIVENESS

In the previous chapter, we examined the importance ascribed by the teachers to a range of educational priorities, specifically as they conceive these priorities within Church of England schools. The educational priorities assessed were grouped within eight broad areas, described as (1) the curriculum, (2) religious education, (3) the Christian community, (4) school ethos, (5) local community, (6) images of the moral life, (7) traditional educational methods and (8) progressive educational methods. Our examination of the importance ascribed to these areas has provided a detailed idea of how the teachers in church schools in a rural diocese conceptualise their function and the kind of educational environment they ideally envisage within their schools. The previous chapter has not, however, enabled us to ascertain the extent to which their views are in any sense directly influenced by the fact that they are teaching in a Church of England school. It is to this question that the present chapter now turns.

The method adopted by this chapter is to retrace the route taken in the previous chapter, but with a new question in mind. Instead of asking the teachers to rate the importance of the range of educational priorities, we shall ask them to assess how much attention they reckon that Church of England schools should give to these goals, compared with county schools. Their assessment of this issue is on a five point scale, ranging from 'much more', through 'a little more', 'the same', and 'a little less' to 'much less'.

As in the previous chapter, we will review the responses of the whole group of teachers first, and then report any significant ways in which the teachers in aided and controlled schools differ from each other in their views. The detailed statistics on which this chapter is based are presented in tables 7.1 through 7.8.

Curriculum

The majority of the teachers are agreed that the basic curriculum should be the same in Church of England schools and county schools. The majority argue that the same attention should be given in Church of England schools and in county schools to physical education (96%), environmental studies (96%), art (95%), maths (94%), english (94%), science (94%), social studies (94%), music (93%) and reading (92%). The small minority not included in these percentages generally tend to argue that everything should be better in church schools than in county schools. For example, they would argue that church schools should, because they are church schools, take maths and english, physical education and all the other school subjects more seriously. This small minority is evenly distributed between those who teach in aided schools and in controlled schools.

The three curriculum components regarding which the teachers agree there should be a different emphasis in Church of England schools and county schools are religious education, moral education and sex education. Thus, 48% of the teachers in controlled schools and 65% of the teachers in aided schools argue that Church of England schools should give more attention to religious education than county schools; 28% of the controlled school teachers and 43% of the aided school teachers argue that Church of England schools should give more attention to moral education than county schools. In the eyes of the teachers, religion and morals go hand in hand as the twin distinctive characteristics of the Church of England school curriculum.

The majority of the teachers (91%) are agreed that the same level of attention should be given to sex education in Church of England schools and county schools. The responses of the teachers who do not agree with this majority position are very interesting. In relationship to all the other curriculum areas on which there is such a majority consensus the minority opinion is clearly in favour of giving more attention within Church of England schools. For example, the 8% of the teachers who do not agree that the same level of attention should be given to reading in Church of England and county schools are unanimous in arguing that Church of England schools should give more attention to the subject. However, when it comes to the matter of sex education, the voice of the minority 9% is clearly divided. In fact, 6% of those who teach in aided schools and 4% of those who teach in controlled schools argue that Church of England schools should give less attention to sex education than county schools.

Religious education

Having argued that Church of England schools should give more attention to religious education than county schools, how in fact do the teachers interpret the significance of this greater attention? What are the distinctive characteristics of the religious education to which more attention is to be given in Church of England schools?

First, the teachers emphasise that church schools should give more emphasis to the Christian religion: 31% believe that Church of England schools should give 'much more' attention than county schools to teaching Christianity. Similarly, in descending order of importance, they argue that much more attention should be given to teaching about Jesus (29%), God (28%), the bible (24%), the church (23%), and church services (20%).

The aided school teachers are much more likely to wish to stress the difference in the emphasis given to religious education in church schools than the controlled school teachers. For example, 75% of the aided school teachers believe that more attention should be given to teaching about Jesus, compared with 56% of the controlled school teachers; 70% of the aided school teachers believe that more attention should be given to teaching about the bible, compared with 50% of the controlled school teachers; 74% of the aided school teachers believe that more attention should be given to teaching children about church services, compared with 59% of the controlled school teachers.

Second, the greater attention which the teachers believe should be given to religious education in church schools is not simply confined to teaching about Christianity. 29% of those who teach in controlled schools and 44% of those who teach in aided schools argue that church schools should also give more emphasis to a careful study of other world religions.

In the previous chapter, we saw that four out of five of the teachers were in favour of integrating religious education with secular subjects. To what extent do they regard such integration as in any sense a particular responsibility of church schools? The answer is that 59% of those who teach in aided schools and 44% of those who teach in controlled schools believe that church schools should be trying harder than county schools to integrate religious education with secular subjects.

Christian community

The previous chapter demonstrated that the majority of the teachers were in favour of church schools reflecting the more general notions of a Christian community. For example, 96% were in favour of conceptualising the school as an appropriate environment in which Christian values should be put into practice; 87% were in favour of providing a regular Christian assembly; 69% were in favour of having religious education taught by a committed Christian] To what extent do the teachers in Church of England schools imagine that these objectives are still appropriate in county schools, and to what extent do they imagine them to be distinctive characteristics of church schools?

While 96% of the teachers argue that they ought to be putting Christian values into practice in church schools, 40% of them would still argue that it is appropriate to do this to the same extent in county schools. Thus, two-fifths of the teachers currently working in church schools still envisage that county schools can function like church schools as an appropriate cradle for Christian values.

〔 Having said this, however, a larger proportion of the teachers (three-fifths) argue that church schools should give more emphasis than county schools to putting Christian values into practice.〕Again, this position is more likely to be adopted by those who teach in aided schools (79%) than those who teach in controlled schools (52%). The same point is reflected in the fact that 63% of the aided school teachers and 49% of the controlled school teachers believe that church schools should give more attention than county schools to providing a regular Christian assembly. Similarly, 68% of the aided school teachers and 46% of the controlled school teachers believe that church schools should give more attention than county schools to saying classroom prayers.

Three-quarters (72%) of the teachers in aided schools and three-fifths (60%) of the teachers in controlled schools believe that church schools should try harder than county schools to provide an atmosphere of Christian community. The majority of the teachers also argue that it is appropriate for church schools to give more attention than county schools to appointing Christians to the teaching staff. Thus, 73% of the aided school teachers and 52% of the controlled school teachers argue that Church of England schools should give more attention to having committed Christians on the staff. Similarly, 63% of the aided school teachers and 52% of the controlled school teachers argue that Church of England schools should give more attention to having religious education taught by a committed Christian.

School ethos

The majority of those who teach in controlled schools do not envisage many significant differences between the ethos of church schools, as defined in the previous chapter, and the ethos of county schools. The majority of these teachers argue that the same emphasis should be given in both church schools and county schools to promoting the pupils' confidence in the staff (92%), to promoting academic attainment (90%), to helping slower pupils (88%), to bringing the best out of bright pupils (88%), to promoting enjoyment of school (87%), to being available to counsel individual children (84%), to respecting each pupil irrespective of ability or appearance (82%) and to creating a caring environment (80%). The majority of the teachers in controlled schools see these goals as educational principles equally shared by church schools and by county schools.

Those who teach in aided schools are more inclined than those who teach in controlled schools to assert the distinctiveness and the excellence of church schools. They place the distinctive elements of the church school ethos in the following descending order of importance. At the top of the list comes the notion of creating a caring environment: more than half of the teachers in aided schools (52%) believe that church schools give more attention to creating a caring environment than county schools. About a third of the teachers in aided schools believe that church schools are better at promoting enjoyment of school (32%), better at respecting each pupil irrespective of ability or appearance (32%) and better at being available to counsel individual children (30%). About a quarter (24%) of the teachers in aided schools believe that church schools are better at promoting the pupils' confidence in the staff. Finally, about a fifth of the teachers in aided schools believe that church schools are better at bringing the best out of bright pupils (18%) and better at helping the slower pupils (22%).

By way of comparison, the majority of those who teach in aided schools do not believe that church schools are characterised by showing more concern than county schools with promoting a high level of academic attainment: 90% of the teachers in aided schools argue that exactly the same level of concern with this issue should be displayed by both church schools and county schools. Just 9% of these teachers argue that church schools should show a higher level of concern with academic attainment than county schools, while 1% of the teachers argue that the reverse should be the case.

Local community

The previous chapter demonstrated that the teachers from both controlled and aided schools placed a high priority on church schools developing close contacts with parents. Those who teach in controlled schools clearly feel that this is a priority they share equally with county schools, and that church schools have little distinctive to offer in this area. Just 11% of the controlled school teachers feel that church schools should give more attention than county schools to knowing about the pupils' home background; 13% feel that church schools should give more attention than county schools to encouraging parents to help in the school; 14% feel that church schools should give more attention than county schools to being available to counsel individual parents; 17% feel that church schools should give more attention than county schools to developing close contacts with parents. In making these assessments, the teachers who work in controlled schools seem to be acknowledging that, in giving priority to these areas, they are simply sharing in the responsibilities accepted by all good schools and not specifically emphasising anything which church schools distinctively offer to educational practice.

While the majority of aided school teachers would also share this general view, a significantly larger minority of them, almost one-third, wishes to emphasise that church schools can operate more effectively in these areas than county schools. Thus, 31% of the aided school teachers argue that church schools can give more attention to knowing about the pupil's home background; 31% argue that teachers in church schools can be more available to counsel individual parents; 30% argue that church schools are more inclined to encourage parents to help in the school; and 29% argue that church schools give more attention to developing close contacts with parents.

Next, we turn attention from contact with parents to examining the teachers' perceptions of contact with the wider local community. Between 97% and 98% of teachers in both controlled and aided schools believe that it should be a priority of Church of England schools to develop close contacts with the local community. Moreover, 31% of the teachers in controlled schools and 41% of the teachers in aided schools believe that church schools should give a higher degree of attention to this priority than county schools.

As may well be expected, the aspect of the contact with the local community which the teachers believe to be specially distinctive of church schools is contact with the clergy. Again the teachers from aided schools give a higher emphasis to the distinctiveness of this priority than the teachers from controlled schools. Thus, about four out of every five of the teachers in aided schools feel that church schools should give more attention than county schools both to developing close contacts with the clergy and to encouraging regular visits from the clergy. In the case of controlled schools, about three out of every five teachers agree with this point of view.

Images of the moral life

We saw from the earlier section on the curriculum that about one in four of the teachers in controlled schools believes that the church school should pay more attention to moral education than the county school. A similar proportion of the teachers in controlled schools (24%) argue that the church school should give more attention to teaching children to live moral lives. However, the image of the moral life which these teachers envisage being taught in church schools does not differ all that greatly from the image of the moral life they envisage being taught in county schools. The majority of the teachers in controlled schools expect the same moral standards to be conveyed in church and county schools, the only difference being that between one in ten and one in five of the teachers imagines that slightly more emphasis should be placed on these moral standards in church schools. Thus, the minority believe that more emphasis should be placed in church schools than in county schools on teaching children to be tidy (8%), training children in hard work (11%), teaching children to obey rules (12%), training children to think for themselves (13%), teaching children good manners (17%), training children in self-discipline (17%), teaching children to be honest and truthful (19%), and teaching children to accept others (19%).

The earlier section on the curriculum also demonstrated that two-fifths of the teachers in aided schools believe that church schools should pay more attention to moral education than county schools. Once again, a similar proportion of the teachers in aided schools (41%) argue that church schools should give more attention to teaching children to live moral lives. This difference in emphasis between teachers in controlled and aided schools is reflected throughout their assessment of the individual moral priorities. Across the board, the aided school teachers believe that church schools should be doing more to promote the moral life, both in the sense of promoting moral self-discipline and in the sense of encouraging obedience to rules. For example, 29% of the teachers in aided schools believe that church schools should be doing more than county schools to train children in self-discipline, compared with 17% of the teachers in controlled schools. On the other hand, 20% of the teachers in aided schools believe that church schools should be doing more than county schools to teach children to obey rules, compared with 12% of the teachers in controlled schools.

Overall, about half (47%) of the teachers in church schools believe that church schools should be doing more than county schools by way of training children to go to church regularly. Once again, the aided school teachers (62%) are more inclined to adopt this point of view than the controlled school teachers (40%).

Traditional methods

The majority of the teachers in church schools do not feel that decisions in favour or against traditional educational methods should be much influenced by the church relatedness of their school. On average, nine out of ten of the teachers argue that the same priority should be given to these traditional methods in both church and county schools. For example, this view applies to regular spelling tests (94%), regular maths tests (94%), regular timetable for different lessons (94%), expecting children to seek permission before leaving the classroom (92%), teaching children to know their multiplication tables by heart (92%), correcting most spelling and grammatical errors (91%), teaching children to write clearly (90%), giving stars or credits for good work (89%), punishing children for persistent disruptive behaviour (88%), adopting firm discipline (87%), adopting strict discipline (86%) and streaming according to ability (86%).

The minority of the teachers, who believe that the emphasis in relationship to these traditional educational methods should be different in church schools and county schools, tend to believe that church schools should place a higher value on the traditional methods. The previous chapter demonstrated that the teachers in aided schools tend to favour traditional educational methods slightly more highly than the teachers in controlled schools. This difference is also reflected in the fact that the minority of the teachers who believe that an emphasis on the traditional educational methods should be a distinguishing characteristic of church schools tend themselves to be located in aided schools. For example, 16% of the aided school teachers believe that church schools should give more attention than county schools to adopting a strict discipline, compared with 9% of the controlled school teachers.

On the other hand, there is also a second clear minority voice which argues that the difference between church schools and county schools should be in a direction away from formal educational methods. For example, from the 14% of the teachers who argue that church schools should take a distinctive stand on streaming according to ability, 8% argue that this stand should be against such streaming, while 6% argue that this stand should be in favour of such streaming. Similarly, from the 11% of the teachers who argue that church schools should take a distinctive stand on giving stars or other credits for good work, 6% argue that this stand should be against such credits, while 5% argue in their favour.

Progressive methods

Just as the majority of the teachers in church schools do not feel that decisions about traditional educational methods should be much influenced by the church relatedness of their school, so they also tend to feel that decisions for and against progressive methods should be made independently of church related issues. Again, on average, nine out of ten of the teachers argue that the same priority should be given to these progressive methods in church schools and in county schools. For example, this view applies to generally allowing children to talk to one another (94%), adopting an integrated day (93%), generally allowing children to move around the classroom (93%), following a project approach to learning (92%), generally allowing children to decide where they sit (90%) and encouraging self-expression (87%).

The minority of the teachers, who believe that the emphasis in relationship to these progressive educational methods should be different in church schools than county schools, tend to divide evenly, half suggesting that church schools should be more progressive than county schools, and half suggesting that they should be less progressive. The one major exception to this consensus concerns the issue of encouraging self-expression. Here the weight of the opinion of those who feel that church schools should be distinctive, is clearly in the direction of encouraging self-expression. Thus, 20% of the teachers in aided schools and 9% of the teachers in controlled schools argue that church schools should give more attention than county schools to encouraging self-expression among their pupils.

Summary

What this chapter shows is that teachers in church schools in a rural diocese do have clear and consistent notions regarding the ways in which church schools can and cannot differ from county schools. These notions can be summarised within three categories.

First, there is a range of educational issues which teachers in church schools regard as professional educational matters in relationship to which the church-relatedness of their school has little distinctiveness to offer. These educational issues include matters like the secular subjects of the curriculum and the choices for and against progressive or traditional educational methods.

Second, there is a range of religious issues which teachers in church schools regard as being appropriate for different treatment in church schools from the treatment they receive in county schools. These religious issues include not only church related matters like contact with the clergy, denominational assemblies and denominational instruction, but also wider issues like religious education and moral education. The teachers in aided schools are more conscious of the distinctiveness of church schools in this religious area.

Third, there is a range of pastoral issues which teachers in church schools regard both as coming within the proper domain of all schools, and also as being promoted with greater sensitivity and commitment by church schools. These pastoral issues include contact with the local community, being available to counsel individual parents, knowing about the pupils' home background, creating a caring environment and promoting enjoyment of school. Again, teachers in aided schools are more conscious of the distinctiveness of church schools in this pastoral area.

8 ATTITUDE FORMATION

So far, the previous three chapters have examined the opinions of those who teach in rural church first, primary and middle schools about three key areas, namely the church school system, teaching itself, and the distinctiveness of church schools. These chapters have covered a wide range of topics and revealed a large variety of opinions. What I propose to do in the present chapter is to employ some more sophisticated statistical procedures in order to uncover the deeper attitudinal structures underlying the teachers' opinions. The social-psychological theory of attitude scaling enables us both to detect the major trends around which the teachers' opinions tend to constellate, and to understand something about the ways in which various groups of teachers differ from each other in the views they hold.

My re-examination of the information presented in the previous three chapters, with the help of the more sophisticated statistical procedures, suggests that there are three key attitudes underlying the individual teachers' responses to their work in church schools. I will attempt to define these three key attitudes briefly and then return to examine them in greater detail.

The first key attitude represents an overall response to the church school system. Teachers vary greatly in their overall acceptance of the church school system. At one end of this attitudinal continuum are those who are favourably disposed to the church school system and at the other end are those who are unfavourably disposed to the system.

The second key attitude represents the way in which the teachers view the relationship between church schools and county schools. Again, teachers vary greatly in the way in which they understand this relationship. At one end of this attitudinal continuum are those who argue that church schools should be identical with county schools in their ethos and practice, while at the other end are those who assert strongly the distinctiveness of church schools. The point is that those who are most in favour of the church school system are not necessarily those who also wish to assert the greatest distinctiveness of church schools.

The third key attitude represents the way in which the teachers understand their actual role in the classroom. At one end of this attitudinal continuum are those who see their work in terms of what we have already styled traditional educational methods, while at the other end are those who favour progressive educational methods.

Having suggested that many of the differences between the individual teachers can be summarised in terms of these three key attitudinal continua, I now need to take the argument two stages further. First, I need to demonstrate precisely what I mean by these three attitudinal continua: how, in practice, can we recognise them? Second, I need to demonstrate how this extra information about the teachers' attitudinal structure can be of practical use: are we any closer to being able to understand why individual teachers hold the views they do? For example, put in more concrete terms, is it likely that the men and women who teach in church schools see their functions differently? Do the older teachers differ much in their views from the younger teachers? Do those who practise the Christian faith tend to have a different view on the value of church schools from those who are not practising believers?

For or against church schools

The first attitude scale sets out to identify the issues which are best able to distinguish between those teachers who are in favour of the church school system and those who are not in favour of it. The statistical procedures of item analysis selected the sixteen items which most satisfactorily satisfy this question. These items are set out in table 8.1 in the appendix, together with an indication of the way in which they cohere to produce a unidimensional scale. The internal consistency of these items produces an alpha coefficient of .8523, which demonstrates that the items cluster together very satisfactorily to form a cumulative scale.

These sixteen items demonstrate that those who are most in favour of the church school system tend to say things like 'I applied for my present post specifically because it was in a Church of England school', 'Anglican parents should be encouraged to send their children to a Church of England school', and 'the Church of England should develop more secondary/middle/upper schools'. Those who are most hostile to the church school system say things like, 'the Church of England school system has outlived its usefulness', 'Church of England schools should be given over to the state' and 'the Church of England has too many schools'. Closely associated with the individual teachers' stand on these polarising issues are their views on the relationship between church and school and the relationship between religion and education. Those in favour of church schools tend to believe that the school system should teach about the church and encourage pupils to accept and practise the Christian faith, while those against church schools tend to believe that the task of Christian education should rest with the churches and with parents rather than with the school system and that it is inappropriate for schools to ask pupils to participate in signs of religious commitment like worship and prayer.

Since the teachers have responded to each of these items on a five point scale, ranging from five for the most favourable response through one for the most unfavourable response, it is now possible to calculate a cumulative scale score for each teacher by adding together their responses for each of the sixteen items. The sixteen item scale thus produces a range of scores from sixteen through eighty.

Elsewhere in the questionnaire, the teachers were asked to specify the kind of school in which they would actually prefer to teach. If this scale successfully distinguishes between those who are favourable to the church school system and those who are unfavourable towards it, there should be a high correlation between the scores on the scale and stated school preference. This is a way of checking that the scale actually measures what it sets out to measure, and is technically known as a method of confirming 'construct validity'. The results are very satisfactory: those who state their preference as teaching in a Church of England aided school score 65.4 points on the scale; those who opt for a Church of England controlled school score 57.6 points; those who opt for a county school score 49.5 points. Those who say that they have no real preference between a church and county school score 53.8 points, a score higher than those who opt for a county school, but lower than those who opt for a controlled school.

The next stage is to examine how much the individual teachers' attitudes for or against the church school system are related to other factors. The factors I shall take into consideration are age, sex, present teaching grade, pattern of church attendance, the differences between those who teach in aided and in controlled schools, the differences between middle schools and the first or primary schools, and the admissions policy of the school. The statistical procedure used to explore these relationships is known as path analysis. The results are shown in path model one.

Path diagrams show relationships in terms of straight lines and arrow heads. I have followed the convention of locating the outcome variable in which we are interested, the attitude score, at the bottom of the page,

PATH MODEL ONE
Attitude towards the church school system

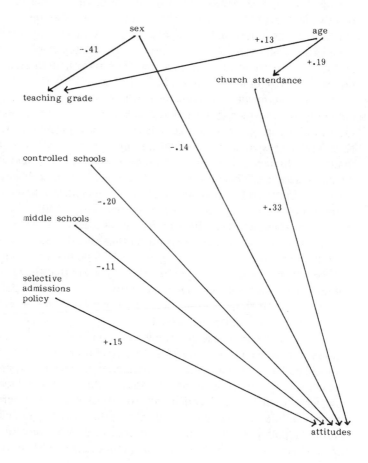

while the variables which are likely to influence the attitude score are listed from the top of the page in the order in which they were entered into the equation. For example, sex and age appear at the top of the page because they are logically prior to all the other factors and not subject to any influence from them. Church attendance comes next as a personal characteristic, and the more specifically job related characteristics follow on from that. This convention means that all the arrow heads logically point down the page. Where downward progressing arrows are not drawn into the diagram, it means that statistically significant relationships do not exist; for example, in path model one no lines appear between age and attitude or between teaching grade and attitude.

We will begin the interpretation of the path diagram by looking at the heading 'teaching grade'. The arrow between age and teaching grade (+.13) confirms the expected outcome that those in more senior posts tend to be older. The arrow between sex and teaching grade (-.41) indicates that the senior posts in church schools tend to go to men.

Church attendance is also positively related to age (+.19). The older teachers in church schools are more inclined to attend church than the younger teachers. No line emerges between sex and church attendence. This is a very interesting point, since, in the population as a whole, women are much more inclined to be church-goers than men. The path model indicates that the men who teach in church schools have the same pattern of church attendance as the women who teach in church schools. In other words, in terms of their religious behaviour, the male teachers in church schools are more likely to be different from the population at large than the female teachers.

The line between church attendance and attitude (+.33) indicates that the teachers who go to church are more likely to be in favour of the church school system than those who do not go to church. Although age influences church attendance and church attendance influences the attitude towards church schools, age itself does not have a direct bearing on attitude towards church schools. This means, for example, that the church-going older teachers will hold a more favourable attitude towards church schools than the non-church-going teachers of the same age, but that there is not necessarily going to be any difference between the attitudes of non-church-going older teachers and of non-church-going younger teachers.

The lack of a line between teaching grade and attitude is also very revealing. This means that those who hold senior posts in church schools are not more likely to have a favourable attitude towards church schools than those of the same age and the same sex who hold junior posts. This indicates that, generally speaking, the allocation of senior posts has neither discriminated in favour of those who support the church school system, nor produced in those who have received promotion a greater degree of support for that system.

The other lines in the path diagram indicate that the female teachers (-.14) tend to be less in favour of the church school system than the male teachers; those who work in controlled schools (-.20) are less in favour of church schools than those who work in aided schools; those who work in middle schools (-.11) are less in favour of church schools than those who work in primary or first schools; those few teachers who work in aided schools which operate a selective admissions policy on religious criteria tend to be more in favour of the church school system than those in the other schools.

One of the strengths of path analysis is the way in which it is able to take all the factors discussed above into account simultaneously. This reduces the risks of error through contaminating influences.

On the basis of the above discussion, it is now possible to draw a profile of those who are most likely and those who are least likely to be in favour of the church school system. Those most in favour of the church school system are male teachers who attend church weekly and who work in aided primary or first schools which operate a selective admissions policy. Those least in favour of the church school system are female teachers who never attend church and who work in controlled middle schools operating an exclusively neighbourhood admissions policy.

Distinctive or not

The second attitude scale sets out to identify the characteristics of church schools which are most likely to be emphasised by those who wish to assert the distinctiveness of the church school. Again, the statistical procedures of item analysis selected the sixteen items which most satisfactorily distinguish between those teachers who say that church schools are or should be different from county schools and those who say that church schools and county schools should be doing exactly the same sort of job, with the same kind of priorities.

Those who wish to emphasise the distinctiveness of church schools tend to talk in terms of the specifically religious characteristics of the school. Right at the top of their list they tend to place the ideas of providing a regular Christian assembly and teaching about Christianity,

God and Jesus. They also consider it important to teach about the bible and the church. They feel that church schools should have committed Christians on the staff and develop close contacts with the local clergy. They believe that prayer has a place in the classroom. They argue that the church school should be a place for putting Christian values into practice and for providing an atmosphere of Christian community.

When these sixteen items are aggregated they also produce a unidimensional scale (see table 8.1), with a range of scores from sixteen through eighty. The internal consistency of these items produces an alpha coefficient of .9445.

The validity of this scale can also be tested against what the individual teachers claim to be their preferred type of school. We might expect those who want to emphasise the distinctiveness of church schools to wish to teach in aided schools, while those who want to stress that church schools should not be distinctive might well see little point in being in a church school. Those who state their preference as teaching in a Church of England aided school score 73.8 points on the scale; those who opt for Church of England controlled schools score 66.3 points; those who opt for a county school score 52.7 points. Those who say that they have no real preference between a church school and a county school score 63.9 points, a score higher than those who opt for a county school, but lower than those who opt for a controlled school.

Path model two which explores the teachers' attitude towards the distinctiveness of church schools assumes a somewhat different shape from path model one. This helps to confirm our notion that attitudes towards the distinctiveness of church schools function independently from attitudes towards the church school system itself. The paths leading to teaching grades and church attendance are, of course, identical in both path models because they are working on the same sets of data.

The first major difference between the two path models is that, in the case of attitudes towards the distinctiveness of church schools, there is a direct path between age and attitude, while this path did not exist in the case of attitudes towards the church school system. While older teachers are not more inclined to be in favour of the church school system, they are more inclined to consider that church schools are or should be different from county schools. Looking more closely at the data, it is the teachers in their fifties or sixties who are most inclined to feel that church schools should be distinctive. This is likely to be a function of the fact that they were trained and served their apprenticeship in a context which was more conscious of the distinctiveness of church

PATH MODEL TWO
Attitude towards the distinctiveness of church schools

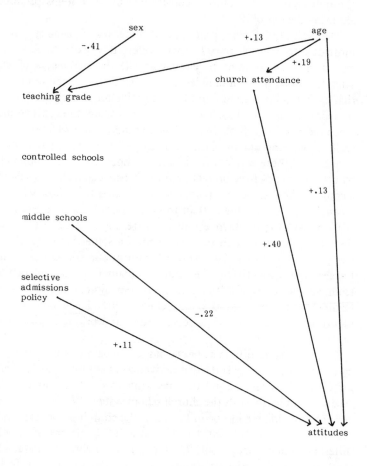

schools than has been the case in more recent years. These are men and women who will remember more clearly the controversy of the religious factor surrounding the 1944 Education Act.

The second major difference is that, in the case of the distinctiveness of church schools, no direct path exists between sex and attitude. While the male teachers were more inclined to be in favour of the church school system, they are not more inclined than the female teachers to wish to emphasise the distinctiveness of church schools.

The third major difference is that no path exists between the controlled schools and attitude towards the distinctiveness of church schools. Although those who work in controlled schools are less likely to be in favour of the church school system than those of the same age and sex who work in aided schools, they are not less likely to support the distinctiveness of church schools.

In three other ways the two path models assume a similar shape. The church attendance of the individual teachers is the strongest predictor of their attitude in both cases. Those who go to church regularly are more likely both to be in favour of the church school system and to emphasise the distinctiveness of church schools. Those who teach in middle schools are less likely to emphasise the distinctiveness of church schools, while those who teach in the aided schools which operate a selective admissions policy on religious grounds are more likely to emphasise the distinctiveness of church schools.

On the basis of the above discussion, it is now possible to draw a profile of those who are most likely and those who are least likely to emphasise the distinctiveness of church schools. Those most likely to emphasise the distinctiveness of church schools are the older men and women who attend church weekly and who work in the kind of aided primary school which operates an admissions policy based on religious criteria. Those least likely to emphasise the distinctiveness of church schools are the younger men and women who never attend church and who work in the middle schools which do not operate an admissions policy based on religious criteria.

Traditional or progressive

The third attitude scale sets out to identify the teaching preferences of those who would characterise themselves as favouring traditional teaching methods, rather than progressive teaching methods. Again, the statistical procedures of item analysis selected sixteen items which most satisfactorily distinguished between those in favour of traditional teaching methods and those in favour of progressive teaching methods. These items are set out in table 8.3 in the appendix, together with an indication of the way in which they cohere to produce a unidimensional scale. The internal consistency of these sixteen items produced an alpha coefficient of .8820, which, once again, is a highly satisfactory index of the scale's reliability and unidimensionality. The cumulative scale scores again range from sixteen through eighty.

Those who value traditional teaching methods place a high priority on teaching children to know their multiplication tables by heart, giving regular maths tests and giving regular spelling tests. They believe in training children in hard work, teaching children to be tidy and adopting firm discipline. They like to follow a regular timetable for different lessons. They emphasise the importance of bringing the best out of bright pupils and of rewarding good work by giving stars and other credit marks. They expect children to seek permission before leaving the classroom, and they expect children to be punished for persistent disruptive behaviour.

The key question now concerns the way in which a preference for traditional teaching methods is likely to be associated with other factors. Are men more or less likely to favour traditional teaching methods than women? Are older teachers more likely to favour traditional teaching methods than younger teachers? Are those who attend church regularly more or less likely to be traditionalists in their approach to teaching? Are those in aided schools any more traditional in their approach than those in controlled schools? Are teachers in middle schools any more traditional in their teaching methods than those in primary or first schools?

Path model three answers each of these questions in the negative. None of these factors is significantly related to the individual's attitude towards traditional teaching methods. Women are just as likely to favour traditional teaching methods as men. Young teachers are just as likely to favour traditional teaching methods as older teachers. Those in first schools are just as likely to favour traditional teaching methods as those in middle schools. Regular church-goers are just as likely to favour traditional teaching methods as those who never go to church. Traditionalists are just as likely to be found in controlled schools as in aided schools and in posts of senior responsibility as in scale one posts.

Having seen that preferences for and against traditional teaching methods are totally unrelated to these other factors, the final question is to examine whether a preference for traditional teaching methods is related to the teacher's attitudes either towards the church school

PATH MODEL THREE
Attitude towards teaching style

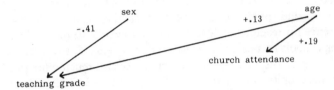

sex

−.41

+.13

age

+.19

church attendance

teaching grade

controlled schools

middle schools

selective
admissions
policy

teaching
style

system or towards the distinctiveness of church schools. Are the teachers who favour traditional teaching methods also likely to favour the church school system or to emphasise the distinctiveness of church schools? This is a very straightforward statistical question for correlational analysis.

The first point to emerge from the correlational analysis is that there is a statistically significant, but very weak relationship between preferences for teaching style and attitude towards the church school system ($r = +.1172$, $P < .05$). Those who favour traditional teaching methods are also slightly more in favour of the church school system.

The second point to emerge is that the relationship between preference for teaching style and attitude towards the distinctiveness of church schools is considerably stronger ($r = +.3246$, $P < .001$). Those who favour traditional teaching methods are also much more in favour of emphasising the distinctiveness of church schools. This suggests that the image of church schools as an environment in which it remains appropriate to emphasise the religious dimension of Christianity is closely associated with a more general tendency to favour traditional teaching methods. At the same time, a relatively independent set of values is operating in determining the teachers' attitudes towards the church school system itself.

While ideas about the religious distinctiveness of church schools may well involve a projection of conservative teaching values onto the church schools issue, these values in no way seriously interact with the individual teachers' arguments for or against the church school system itself. From the teachers' point of view, there is little truth in the notion that church schools are favoured as a final bastion of traditional teaching methods.

Implications

The detailed statistical analysis of this chapter offers some significant pointers regarding the likely future of the church school system in rural areas. If it is true that the character of church schools depends very much upon the attitudes and policies of those who actually teach in them, the church needs to be taking very seriously the views of today's teachers. The church also needs to begin to predict the climate of opinion among the teachers of tomorrow, as the senior members of staff retire, as a new generation of teachers is promoted into headships and as young men and women are recruited into teaching in their first church schools.

The first pointer is provided by the scale of 'attitude towards the church school system' itself. Already we are aware that today only a small proportion of those who teach in church schools specifically chose to be working in the church school system, just 10% of the teachers in controlled schools and 37% of the teachers in aided schools. While the majority of the teachers who find themselves working in the church school system still show considerable goodwill towards that system, their goodwill towards church schools is also clearly associated with their goodwill towards the church in general.

The statistical model suggests that the younger teachers are less likely to be church-goers and that the teachers who are not church-goers are less likely to be favourably disposed towards the church school system. This model could imply that the next generation of teachers in church schools is likely to be less favourably disposed towards the church school system than the present generation. My earlier study, *Rural Anglicanism: a future for young Christians?*, demonstrates the decline in membership of rural churches and highlights the increasing inability of rural churches to attract children, young people and young families into membership. My prediction is that, as young teachers in rural church schools become more alienated from their local churches, so their sympathy for the church school system itself will decline. The puzzle with which the rural churches will be left is making sense of retaining an investment in school sites after the commitment of the teaching staff to the church's involvement in education has worn thin. The signs are that the rural church will have to face this problem soonest in its controlled middle schools.

The second pointer is provided by the scale of 'attitude towards the distinctiveness of church schools'. At present the main emphasis of the teachers who argue in favour of the distinctiveness of church schools specifically concerns the Christian character of these schools. For example, half of the teachers in controlled schools and two-thirds of the teachers in aided schools currently argue that church schools should give more emphasis than county schools to providing a regular Christian assembly. The statistical model clearly suggests that this notion of distinctiveness is not only related to the individual teachers' attitudes towards the church, but also to their age.

In the case of their attitude towards the church school system, younger church-going teachers are just as likely to be favourably disposed to the church's involvement in education as older church-going teachers. It is simply the case that fewer young teachers go to church. In the case of their attitude towards the distinctiveness of church schools, younger church-going teachers are less likely to support the Christian distinctiveness of church schools than older church-going teachers.

This model implies that the belief among teachers in church schools that church schools should be different is likely to disappear more rapidly, as the next generation of church school teachers emerges, than their general goodwill towards the church's continued involvement in education. My prediction is that, as younger teachers replace the more senior members of staff in rural church schools, so the desire to assert the distinctiveness of church schools will decline. The puzzle with which the rural churches will be left is making sense of operating schools which are indistinguishable from comparable neighbourhood county schools. The signs are that the rural church will have to face this problem soonest in its middle schools.

9 INDIVIDUAL PROFILES

The perspective of the preceding chapters has been to make statistical generalisations about the teachers in church schools as a group. This kind of analysis is only part of the story. As well as leading to statistical generalisations, the information collected by the survey also enables us to draw detailed profiles of the individual teachers who co-operated in the project. The chance to look at a few of these profiles in depth can usefully serve to illustrate the richness of the data and remind us that, beneath the generalisations, we are the whole time dealing with uniqueness and individuality. The opportunity to meet a few of these teachers close up brings into sharper perspective the wide range of views held and the important implications of these views for those concerned with the future of the church school system. When all is said and done, it is precisely the views and attitudes of the individual teachers in the specific schools which determine the way in which the church school system is interpreted and implemented in any given situation.

From the 338 detailed questionnaires completed by the teachers in church schools in the diocese, I have selected just seven to form the subject of in-depth profiles. The seven selected include the deputy headteacher of a controlled primary school, Janet Tucker; the headteacher of a small controlled first school in a rural area, Robert Higgins; the headteacher of a small aided primary school in a more urban area, Gordon Todd; two teachers on scale one posts in controlled first schools, Susan Hollings who is at the beginning of her teaching career, and Grace Goodenough who is nearing retirement; Judith Wright who has a scale one post in one of the few aided primary schools in the diocese which admit children mainly on religious criteria; and Philip Wilding who holds a scale two post in one of the four controlled middle schools in the diocese. My aim has been to provide a careful and detailed account of the views held by these seven teachers. While these character profiles are wholly and carefully based on real people, the names attributed to the teachers and to their schools are fictitious.

Janet Tucker

Janet Tucker is the second member of staff in the two-teacher Church of England voluntary controlled primary school at Bloxford. Bloxford is a small community of less than 250 inhabitants. Janet has both lived and worked in this community for more years than she cares to say.

Janet is now in her mid-fifties and has seen a great number of changes take place both in Bloxford village and in her school. The new lady headteacher is a good ten years younger than Janet and lives well outside the school's catchment area. Janet tends to feel that this gives her a greater sense of responsibility for the school since, after all, she is the person who lives in the same community as the children, meets their parents socially in the local church and casually in the village shop, and who knows so much about their individual history and backgrounds. Although technically employed as a scale one teacher, Janet now prefers to describe herself as the deputy headteacher of Bloxford School.

Not only does Janet live in Bloxford, she is a stalwart member of the parish church. As church councillor and churchwarden, Janet faithfully attends all the Sunday church services. Since Bloxford is now part of a multi-parish benefice, this means in practice a mid-morning communion service on the second and fourth Sundays of the month and an evensong on the third Sunday. On the first Sunday of the month Bloxford church co-operates with another parish in the benefice by attending a united family service.

Although Janet represents in herself a strong link between the village school and the local church, she is very conscious that this link does not have many practical implications for the pupils of the school. Bloxford church itself does not organise its services with children particularly in mind and Bloxford children do not generally travel to the neighbouring parish for the monthly united family service.

In spite of the fact that the relationship between church and school does not work out as fruitfully as Janet would wish to see it, she remains very positively committed to the church school system. In particular she believes in the controlled school system. Her vision of a church school is a village school serving every child in the neighbourhood in exactly the same way as a county school, only doing the job so much better. While she believes that church-going parents stand in particular to benefit from such schools, she does not feel that they should in any sense restrict their intake to the children of church-going families.

Before coming to Bloxford Church of England Voluntary Controlled School, Janet had only taught in county schools. At the time when she applied for her present job, she did not specifically apply for her post because it was a church school. However, since coming to Bloxford she has become more and more appreciative of the church school system. She is now convinced that, given the choice and all things being equal, she would generally prefer to teach in a Church of England controlled school.

As far as she can see, church schools do not deserve the kind of criticisms they sometimes receive. There is no sense in which Bloxford School could be regarded as either socially or racially divisive, since it serves its neighbourhood just like any other school. Such a school does not seem to confer unfair privileges either to pupils or staff.

Thinking back to the recent appointment of the new headteacher, Janet feels that this confirms the fact that church schools do not give unfair advantages to Christian teachers in the promotion stakes. On the contrary, she rather wishes that church schools took greater care to recruit church people onto the staff. She increasingly feels that only committed church people should be appointed to teach in a Church of England school. In order to make the best use of the church school system, she argues that teachers should receive special initial training to equip them for work in church schools and that this should be followed up by special in-service training. At present, she feels that there is a lack of qualified and effective teachers of religion in Church of England schools. She argues that the Roman Catholic church makes a much better job of selecting staff for Roman Catholic church schools.

Janet's ideas about the purposes of the church school system are particularly tailored to the primary sector. While she believes that the Church of England should continue to maintain its present level of involvement in the provision of rural church primary schools, she feels that church schools make much less sense for secondary aged pupils. The important feature of the controlled primary school for Janet is its church-related nature, rather than its specifically Anglican identity. She believes that the future for church primary schools should lie much more in the interdenominational sphere.

Janet has some very clear ideas about how a church school should differ from a county school and she has no doubt that these differences make church schools superior in terms both of the education they provide and the overall care they give to their pupils.

Janet belongs to the progressive rather than the traditional school of educational theory and practice. She believes in the integrated day rather than the strict timetabling of different lessons. She believes in the project approach to learning. She feels that it is important to encourage self expression and to give pupils the freedom to move around the classroom. She is very much against the formal method of giving regular maths tests and spelling tests. She rejects the ideas of attempting to stream according to ability or of rewarding good conduct with stars or other credits. She wants her english lessons to encourage creative writing, rather than neatly formed letters, correct spelling and good grammar.

For Janet one of the obvious strengths of church schools is that they should enable teachers to follow more progressive educational methods. She believes that discipline should be more relaxed in a church school and that teachers should give pupils more encouragement. She believes that church schools should create less competition among pupils and draw less attention to the distinctions between the bright and the less able children. Church schools should be more patient with disruptive pupils.

Janet believes that in the primary school curriculum goals like art, music and environmental studies should rank in importance alongside reading and creative writing, and be placed even above maths. Again, she feels that these are curriculum priorities which are more likely to reach expression in the church school, where subjects like music and art can be more highly valued.

Moral education and religious education also rank among Janet's top curriculum priorities, and these also are subjects to which she reckons that church schools are able to give greater emphasis.

The kind of religious education which Janet values is very much a bible-based form of Christianity. She feels that schools should concentrate on teaching the stories of God and Jesus drawn from scripture. Although a regular church-goer herself, she does not feel that the primary school is the proper place to teach pupils about church services. While she believes it is right and appropriate for church schools to give more time and emphasis than county schools to bible teaching, she does not believe that church schools should give more time than county schools to teaching specifically about the church and about church services.

Janet believes that the aims of religious education in church schools should be the same as those in county schools. She happily endorses the idea that school religious education "should help children to understand what religion is and what it would mean to take a religion seriously". She argues that good religious education should not involve denominational teaching and she strongly discourages the idea of teaching pupils about the communion service in school.

Having said all this, however, Janet is far from abandoning the confessional purposes of religious education. The bible stories which she tells to her pupils are far from being seen purely as objective religious phenomena. While she acknowledges that home is more important than school in determining the child's religious commitment, she does not believe that the whole job of Christian education can be left to the parents and to the churches. She argues that it is part of the school's job to encourage pupils to accept and to practise the Christian faith. While she sees that church schools should be particularly good at achieving this, she reckons that county schools should be working towards the same end as well.

Because in today's society many of the pupils are not introduced to the Christian faith at home, Janet believes that it is even more important for the schools to do this job. In particular she feels that pupils should be introduced to the habits of prayer and worship through a regular Christian assembly and through classroom prayers. Again she feels that church schools are able to give more priority to this side of life than county schools, although at the same time she emphasises that it is not so much what church schools do that make them different, but the excellence with which they do it.

Janet believes that there is a very close relationship between religion and morality and for this reason she reckons that church schools can do a better job in the area of moral education. Church schools, she believes, can give more time to teaching children to live moral lives, to teaching children to accept others and to helping them to become honest and truthful.

Janet's ideas about the distinctiveness of church schools do not stop with the curriculum. She believes that one of the most important features of church schools is the way in which they can provide an atmosphere of Christian community and a context in which Christian values can be put into practice. Ideally, Janet sees the church school as providing an exemplary caring environment which shows respect for each individual pupil, irrespective of ability or appearance. In particular, the atmosphere of the church school should be able to help the slower and more disadvantaged pupils. Teachers in church schools should be available to counsel individual children and to help them get the most out of their time at school.

Janet believes that rural primary schools are ideally suited for being able to develop close contacts between the school and the rest of the community. She believes that it is important for schools to know as much as possible about the pupils' home backgrounds and to develop close contacts with parents. She wants to encourage parents to help in the school and for the school to be available to help individual parents. Again, Janet believes that church schools are in a much stronger position to build up these close links between school and community.

In particular, Janet values the way in which church schools are able to develop links with the local clergy. She believes that it is important for the clergy to be made welcome in the school and for the clergy to be able to get to know the children of the community through the school.

Although Janet likes and respects the local vicar, she is frustrated by his failure to make a real contribution to the life of the school. She recognises that the vicar tries to take an active interest in what is going on in the school, but Janet very much wishes that he did not feel so much out of his depth when talking with children. The problem, she says, is that clergy are not properly trained for their work in church schools. They are not generally aware of current educational thinking and are therefore not competent to take lessons. Sometimes the vicar of Bloxford takes the morning assembly; Janet longs to help him to make a better job of doing so, but she does not know where to begin in achieving this.

Where the vicar makes his best contribution to the life of the school is through his role as chairman of the school governors. While many of the other governors seem to be very distant from the school, the vicar at least often visits the school and has regular contact with the two teachers between governors' meetings. She wishes that the other governors would come into the school from time to time and give the pupils the opportunity to get to know them.

In part, Janet blames the diocese for the lack of significant contact between her school and the local church. She feels that the diocese could do so much more to help the clergy and governors to understand and to fulfil their job better. On her side Janet would be only too delighted to work more closely with the diocese in fulfilling her vision for the place of church schools in today's society.

Thus, in Janet we meet a teacher who is very committed to the distinctiveness and excellence of church schools. Her commitment to church schools flows directly from her twin commitments to her church and to the development of her pupils. Through teachers like Janet, the church has been enabled to establish its credibility in rural primary education. The big question mark, however, comes if it should no longer be seen to be appropriate, in a secular state maintained educational system, for Christian teachers to project so clearly the implications of their faith on to their professional conduct.

Robert Higgins

Robert Higgins is the headteacher of a small Church of England voluntary controlled first school situated in the centre of Great Tickwell, a picturesque village. The school still occupies its Victorian buildings in the shadow of the parish church. Robert is in his forties, and this is his first headship.

Robert says that he is very committed to the church school system, although it is really a matter of chance that he finds himself currently teaching in a church school. At the stage when he was looking for a headship, the present post was advertised; he applied and was offered the post. The fact that Great Tickwell school was a church school in no way influenced his decision to put in an application for the post. He would have applied just the same had it been a county school. All things being equal, Robert would really prefer to be teaching in the independent sector, but the right opening has never come his way.

Although he feels that he is committed to the church school system, Robert is not himself committed to the Christian church. He does not regard himself as belonging to any specific church, although he would classify himself as 'sympathetic to religion'. He usually attends church somewhere once or twice a year, but not more regularly. He never worships in the parish church next to his school, but he does not live in the parish either.

Robert firmly believes that religion should play a central part in the life of schools, and by that he means in the life of county schools as well as church schools. He supports the confessionalist view that it is not inappropriate for county schools to try to initiate children into a religious faith. He is even clear that church schools have an open mandate to try to convert children to believe in Christianity. He reckons that there should be a distinctively Christian view of education, and he sees no difficulties in schools expecting children to engage in prayer and worship, in spite of the fact that they might never engage in such activities at home. In fact, Robert believes that the school can often be more important than home in determining the child's religious commitment. He certainly does not accept the idea that Christian education should be the prerogative of homes and churches, rather than schools.

He believes that church schools should give more emphasis to religious education than county schools, but he reckons that religious education in church schools should still be non-denominational. The aim of this religious education should be to encourage the pupils to accept Christianity, not to become members of a specific church. With this end in mind, he believes that it is right for church schools to teach their pupils about the communion service, but not for the communion to be celebrated in school.

Robert feels that church schools are not doing enough to teach religion these days and that there is a serious lack of qualified and effective teachers of religion in church schools generally. He says that "the main disappointment I have when meeting church school colleagues to discuss RI is the air of apology that seems to accompany anyone's confession to actually be doing some unadulterated RI from the bible. No such air of apology accompanies the majority, however, when they say what 'RI' they have been doing, church history, architecture, village environment, models of the church - in fact anything except real RI". In spite of this dissatisfaction with the way in which he feels that religious education is currently taught in church schools, Robert does not believe that there is any need for the diocese to give more help to the subject, or that there is a need for new or better teaching materials to be developed for the subject. He sees no need for special in-service training programmes; nor does he feel that greater care should be given to the selection of staff for church schools. Robert has put his finger on what he would describe as an urgent problem, but he sees no way towards its remedy.

Robert is also very critical of the way in which the diocese and the church as a whole relates to church schools. He reckons that the Church of England does not take enough interest in church schools and that the diocese should take more responsibility for fostering links between schools and local churches. All told, he feels that the Roman Catholic Church makes a much better job of running church schools than the Church of England.

At a more local level, Robert criticises the foundation governors for not taking enough interest in their church school. He feels that foundation governors do not have an adequate understanding of the role of schools today and that they do not involve themselves sufficiently in the life of the school. He feels that the local vicar is as guilty of this neglect of the school as the other foundation governors. However, at another level, he is quite grateful that the vicar does not take a more active part in the life of the school. Robert feels that the real work of the school is his responsibility and that the vicar is only likely to get in the way if he were to take a greater interest. He does not encourage the vicar to teach in the school and he is far from convinced of the vicar's qualifications or ability to do so. On the other hand, the vicar does take an occasional assembly and generally Robert feels that he makes a good job of doing so.

Robert is aware that church schools can come in for a lot of criticism from those who wish to see a greater state control over education, but he feels that these criticisms are largely unjustified. He does not believe that church schools are either socially or racially divisive; nor does he consider that they confer unfair privileges to some children. At the same time, he denies that church schools give unfair advantages to Christian teachers in the promotion stakes. Looking at the question from the church's point of view, he reckons that there are no grounds for the criticism that church schools are often counter-productive and actually turn pupils away from the church.

Robert is convinced that, far from withdrawing from the church school system, the Church of England should actually strengthen its hand in education. Although he would not encourage the founding of new village first or primary schools, he believes the church would be wise to encourage some of its controlled first and primary schools to explore the possibility of gaining aided status. At the same time, he believes that the Church of England should try to develop more secondary/middle/upper schools. Robert's belief in the future of church schools is firmly committed to their denominational character. He does not approve of the idea of developing interdenominational Christian schools.

While continuing to believe firmly in the church school system, Robert believes that some serious thought should be given to the purpose of these schools. It seems to him that church schools should not be content just to operate on a neighbourhood admissions policy identical to county schools. Although he does not want to see church schools existing solely to serve the needs of practising Anglicans, or even church-goers from a wider range of denominational backgrounds, he feels that church schools should be giving priority to the children of church-goers. At the same time, he feels that Anglican parents should be encouraged to send their children to a Church of England school, even if this is not the school closest to their home. Because of their church foundation, Robert also feels that church schools should be able to give priority to children with special needs and who require a particularly high level of attention or care.

As a teacher, Robert is clearly in favour of a tradionalist approach to teaching. He believes in teaching his pupils to know their multiplication tables by heart. He believes in streaming according to ability, and adopting a strict discipline. He believes that children should be punished for disruptive behaviour. He gives regular spelling tests and regular maths tests; and he issues stars for good work. At the same time, he comes out strongly against notions like project learning and the integrated day. He does not believe in allowing children to move around the classroom, to decide for themselves where they want to sit, or to talk to one another in class.

Robert believes that this traditionalist approach to teaching should be one of the hallmarks of the church school. Generally speaking, he reckons that the church school should give more attention to teaching multiplication tables, streaming according to ability, giving regular maths tests, issuing stars for good work, and so on. At the same time, he feels that church schools should give less attention to things like project learning, the integrated day and an informal teaching atmosphere and environment.

The subjects which Robert rates most highly are maths, reading, moral education and religious education. He also values, although less highly, subjects like music, art, social studies and physical education. He does not feel that areas like science and environmental studies should be regarded as all that important in the primary school. He feels very strongly that sex education should not appear in the school curriculum at all.

Generally, Robert feels that the curriculum priorities of church schools should be identical with those of county schools, but he also believes that there should be two major exceptions to this. First, he believes that church schools should give much more emphasis to religious education and moral education. Second, he believes that church schools should give less emphasis to the less academic components of the curriculum, like music and art.

The kind of religious education which Robert envisages gives the highest priority to teaching about Jesus and the bible. He feels that teaching about God and the church is also important, but less so. Robert is not in favour of the primary school teaching about world religions; nor is he in favour of integrating religious education with secular subjects. He wants to see religious education remain as a distinctive bible-based component in the school timetable. Robert's view of religious education in the church school is that it should cover the same ground as religious education in the county school, but that there should be much more of it.

The kind of moral education which Robert envisages places a high emphasis on training children to obey external moral rules and to be obedient to authority figures. He argues that it is the job of the school to teach children good manners, to be honest and truthful, and to be tidy. He reckons that church schools should make greater efforts in these directions than county schools.

Robert sees the Christian character of church schools being reflected primarily in their religious education, moral education and daily assemblies. In addition to this, he feels that church schools should provide an atmosphere of Christian community and be places where Christian teachers put Christian values into practice.

The most important goal of church schools, according to Robert, is to promote a high level of academic attainment. He feels that church schools should give more attention to this goal even than county schools. He also believes that church schools should help the slower pupils, but that they should be giving no more emphasis to this than county schools. Robert does not believe that it is the job of church schools to set out to create a particularly caring environment, or that it is the job of the staff in church schools to be available to counsel individual children or their parents. First and foremost, he sees schools to be places to which children come to learn and consequently he locates the pupils' actual enjoyment of school very low on his list of educational priorities. Indeed he feels that the idea of promoting the pupils' enjoyment of school should take a lower place in the priority structure of church schools than of county schools.

Robert is not all that conscious of the relationship between his school and the community it serves. He does not place a high priority on developing contacts with the local community, or even with the parents of his pupils. He does not feel that it is particularly important to know about the pupils' home backgrounds. Although his is a church school, Robert does not feel that it is important or sensible to encourage close contacts with the clergy. In fact, Robert feels that a church school has no more responsibility to form relationships with the local clergy, or with the local community at large, than a county school.

Thus, in Robert, we meet a headteacher of a Church of England controlled first school who believes that he is very highly committed to the church school system. However, his commitment to the system is a reflection of his conservative values rather than a result of a commitment to the Christian church or a reflective theology of education. The church-relatedness of his school seems to have become just another justification for clinging to a particular view of education which Robert has adopted for a whole range of personal and professional reasons. Perhaps, after all, he would be happier working not in a Church of England controlled first school, but in a highly formal and traditionally orientated independent school.

Gordon Todd

Gordon Todd is the headteacher of the Church of England voluntary aided primary school in Loddington, one of the small towns in the diocese. Although it is a town in which there is also a county primary school, this aided school understands its role primarily as serving a neighbourhood function for part of Loddington, rather than as offering a specifically Christian alternative for those parents throughout the whole of Loddington who want a church-related education for their children.

Gordon feels very strongly that what should be distinctive about church schools is neither their admissions policy nor their curriculum, but the recruitment of committed Christians to the teaching staff. This is Gordon's first headship. After teaching in both county and Church of England controlled schools, Gordon says that he deliberately set out to find his first headship in a Church of England aided school. He would not have applied for the post in Loddington had it been a county school.

Gordon's view of being head of a Church of England aided school is that he should take an active part in the life of the parish church to which the school is associated. He moved house in order to live in the parish. Most Sundays he is to be found in the congregation of the parish church.

Gordon feels that his own attitude towards the responsibility of being headteacher of a church school is not one which many of his colleagues would share, and he regrets this fact. He feels that greater care should be taken in making appointments to church schools to assure that committed church people are appointed. He feels, too, that church school teachers could benefit from both some special initial training and in-service training programmes. He also feels that controlled school status is not particularly helpful to the church and that ways should be found for helping controlled schools to change to aided status.

Overall, Gordon feels very committed to the church school system. Far from considering gradual withdrawal from the state maintained sector of education, Gordon believes that the Church of England should strengthen its investment in schools, even when this will involve stretching the church's financial resources. In particular, he feels very strongly that the Church of England should attempt to develop more secondary schools. It seems to Gordon that the Roman Catholic Church is currently giving a much more positive lead in education than the Church of England, and he would like to see the Church of England take the Roman Catholic Church's example more seriously. In many ways he reckons that the path ahead might lie in the direction of developing new ecumenical schools.

While Gordon is aware that a number of people are critical of the church school system, he feels that the majority of their criticisms are really unfounded. Nothing in his experience suggests that church schools are either racially or socially divisive. Similarly, in his experience church schools have not discriminated in favour of appointing Christian teachers to posts of responsibility. He concludes that, in principle, church schools might give unfair privileges to some children, say the children of church-going parents, but he feels that church schools have a real responsibility to make sure that this does not happen in practice.

In order to avoid these kinds of criticism, Gordon believes that it is important that Church of England aided schools should admit children from the immediate neighbourhood catchment area in precisely the same way as county schools. He feels that it is wrong for church schools to give any preference to children from church-going or Anglican families. Nor does he believe that it is right for Anglican parents to wish to find separate schools for their children. Because of the way in which he sees the close identity between the school and the neighbourhood in which it is located, Gordon does not go along with the notion that church schools should try to provide special facilities for children with particular needs from a wider area.

Although Gordon envisages church schools admitting all the children from a given neighbourhood in exactly the same way as county schools, he still believes that church schools have a clear mandate to treat the religious education of their pupils as if they came from practising Christian homes. He believes that it is quite appropriate for the aims of religious education in county schools and in church schools to be different, in spite of the fact that they are likely to be dealing with an identical intake of pupils. While he concedes that it is not the task of county schools to initiate children into a religious faith, he feels that it is quite appropriate for Church of England schools to encourage pupils to accept and practise Christianity. He sees no problems in attempting to mix education and evangelism in church schools, and to do so on the firm basis of denominational teaching.

In some ways, Gordon agrees that the home is often more important than the school in determining the child's religious commitment, but he feels that it would be wrong if church schools were to deny their own responsibility for communicating the Christian faith. While many children might never experience praying at home, Gordon reckons that the church school has a responsibility to encourage them to engage in prayer and worship while at school. Going beyond this, he also feels that it is appropriate for children in church schools to participate in the communion service celebrated at school.

Gordon feels that a good relationship exists between his school and the local church. The local vicar makes a real effort to visit the school and to take an interest in what is going on in the school. He is a good chairman to the school governors and the children seem to respond well to him. Generally the pupils enjoy and appreciate the classes and assemblies taken by the vicar. At the same time, Gordon is aware of quite a gulf between the vicar's views on education and those of himself and his professional teaching staff. Gordon argues that the problem is that clergy often do not have the professional background and training to become properly involved in their church schools.

While he is appreciative of the interest taken by the vicar in his school, Gordon is not so complimentary of the other foundation governors. He feels very strongly that the majority of the foundation governors do not take enough interest in the school. They hardly ever visit the school; and when they do visit they have very little idea of their responsibilities or of the educational aims of the school.

Looking beyond his own situation, Gordon feels that the Church of England as a whole is very neglectful of its church schools. He very much appreciates the help given within the diocese by the diocesan education team, and by the religious education adviser in particular. On the other hand, he feels that more initiative could be taken at a national level by the Church of England, especially in relationship to the development of curriculum materials. In short, he believes that church schools could do with much more help than they actually receive from the Church of England.

As a teacher, Gordon takes up a middle of the road position on the debate between progressive and traditional educational methods. He favours many of the characteristics of the progressive approach: he believes in generally allowing children to move around the class and to talk with each other; he believes in the integrated day and in the project approach to learning. On the other hand, he also believes in teaching children to know their multiplication tables by heart; he believes in an overall firm discipline and in punishing children for persistent disruptive behaviour. Gordon is quite clear that decisions on these issues should not be influenced by the fact that he is teaching in a church school. He would adopt precisely the same attitudes to teaching were he working in a county school.

As far as the curriculum is concerned, Gordon attributes exactly the same levels of importance to all the major teaching subjects. He rates maths, english, science, music, art, environmental studies, physical education, moral education, and religious education as all standing on an equal footing. Again, he believes that curriculum priorities should be determined irrespective of whether the school is church-related. Even in the cases of religious education and moral education, he argues that church schools should give exactly the same emphasis as county schools.

Looking more closely at the content of religious education in the church school, Gordon believes that equal attention should be given to teaching about world religions as to teaching about Jesus, the bible, Christianity and the church. He is also very much in favour of integrating religious education with secular subjects. The only way in which he envisages the content of religious education being different in church schools from county schools is that he believes that church schools should give more attention to teaching about church services.

The moral education which Gordon advocates for the Church of England primary school is also the same as that which he would advocate for a county school. He sees the aims of moral education in quite traditional terms: to involve teaching children good manners, to be tidy, to work hard and to obey rules.

Sex education is something about which Gordon is far from happy in the primary school. He reckons that it is a mistake to give much attention to sex education at this age. Again, he feels that church schools and county schools should be equally reticent on this issue.

Gordon feels that it is the job of the primary school to provide an atmosphere of Christian community. He is convinced that this should be a priority equally for county schools and for church schools. He feels it is important for all schools to have committed Christians on the staff, for religious education to be taught by committed Christians, and for teachers to try to put Christian values into practice in the schools. By taking these things seriously, Gordon believes that church schools would be doing nothing more than good county schools.

As part of this Christian community, Gordon believes that it is the duty of all schools to provide a regular Christian assembly and to encourage the practice of saying classroom prayers. Where he feels that the responsibility of church schools and county schools part company is in relationship to the more specifically denominational aspects of the Christian community. He argues that it is not consistent with the brief of county schools to hold school communion services or to prepare pupils for confirmation, but he reckons that church schools should be doing these things.

The more general aspects of the ethos of the school are also seen by Gordon to be unrelated to whether or not the school is of a church foundation. His own view is that the school ethos should try to strike the right balance between promoting academic attainment and promoting the pupils' enjoyment of school.

Gordon believes that it is very important for the primary school to develop close contacts with the local community of which it is part. He believes it is important for the school to know as much as possible about the pupils' home backgrounds. He believes that the school should encourage regular visits from parents and, indeed, encourage parents to help in the school as much as possible. He wants to be available to help and to counsel individual parents when they come seeking help. He also believes that it is important to encourage the clergy to have close contacts with the schools in their parishes. Again, he feels that it is equally important and appropriate for the clergy to take an interest in their local county schools as in their local church schools.

Thus, in Gordon we meet a headteacher of a Church of England aided primary school who is himself a practising churchman highly committed to the Christian faith. He is totally in favour of the church school system, and sees that system as giving the church the opportunity to share with the state the function of educating the nation's children. His views on the Christian nature of county schools are, however, becoming increasingly anachronistic. Given the secularisation of county schools, Gordon will soon find himself having to radically rethink his understanding of the potential distinctiveness of church schools.

Susan Hollings

Susan Hollings is a young woman in her first teaching job after leaving college. She is working in the Church of England voluntary controlled first school at Woolstock.

When she was coming to the end of her initial training, Susan's main concern was to find a job in a primary school. She had never given much thought to the differences between county schools and church schools, and she hardly noticed that Woolstock was a church school when she first applied. Even now she is not sure whether it is an aided school or a controlled school, and she does not know what the difference would be between them anyway.

Now that she finds herself actually teaching in a church school, Susan has reached the conclusion that she feels strongly against the church school system. She has come to believe that the church school system has outlived its usefulness and that the Church of England should take every step to withdraw from its involvement in the state maintained sector of education as soon as possible. She believes that aided schools and controlled schools should be given over to the county.

Susan has come to this conclusion, not because she does not regard herself as a Christian believer, but because she feels that we are no longer generally living in a Christian society. She says that "I feel Church of England schools, as they exist at the moment, are inappropriate in our multi-ethnic society. Most of the children at my school are from homes that do not go to church regularly. This being the case, I feel that much of the religious teaching we give is of little value because it is not backed at home by parents".

The main criticism which Susan voices against church schools is that they tend to be racially divisive, although this does not happen to be a real problem in Woolstock, where the school admits all children from the neighbourhood and where there are no ethnic minority families anyway. On the other hand, Susan does not want to criticise church schools for being socially or educationally divisive; nor does she feel that the dual system creates unfair advantages for Christian teachers in the promotion stakes.

Although not a great church-goer, Susan regards herself as a member of the Church of England and she generally tries to attend services at the major Christian festivals, like Easter, Christmas and Harvest Festival. She believes that the churches should have a real responsibility to communicate the Christian faith to children, but that they should not try to do this through day schools. She believes that it is wrong to try to mix education and evangelism, and that day schools should not set out to initiate children into a religious faith. She argues that "those parents to whom religious education is important, should undertake much of this education in the individual home situation, and could, if necessary, ask for extra help from the church". She feels that instead of being involved in day schools the churches should develop the Sunday school system "to provide thirty minutes of good and organised religious education rather than forty-five minutes of 'all things bright and beautiful' and colouring pictures".

Consequently, Susan reckons that the religious education given by church schools should be identical to that given by county schools. The aim of this religious education should not be to encourage pupils to accept and practise the Christian faith; nor should it involve denominational teaching. Instead, she approves highly the idea that religious education should set out to "help children to understand what religion is and what it would mean to take a religion seriously". Susan has thoroughly absorbed the theories about religious education which were being advocated in her college training during the 1970s. Similarly, she feels that it is wrong for schools to expect children to pray and to engage in worship. On Susan's account, this is not consistent with what education should be about in a secular age.

Against this background, Susan feels that, if church schools are to continue to exist, they should operate as much as possible along the same lines as county schools. They should cease to offer anything distinctive by way of religious education, and they should not attempt to operate any form of admissions policy on religious criteria. Church schools should not give preference to the children of Anglicans or church-going families; nor should Christian parents be encouraged to seek a different form of schooling for their children. Church schools should admit children from the neighbourhood, just like county schools.

Because she does not believe in the distinctiveness of church schools in any sense, Susan can see no point in there being particular contact between the individual school and the diocese, or, indeed, between the school and the local church. She feels that the diocese and the local church should leave the school well alone to get on with its job of educating children like any other school.

Since arriving at Woolstock school, Susan has had very little contact with the governors, and she is not at all sure which of the governors represent the church and which represent other bodies. Generally, she feels that the governors seem to take very little interest in the school, and that they do not really seem to undertand the job of schools today anyway.

Susan is aware that the vicar is one of the governors. She is far from sure that it is a good idea to have the clergy involved in schools in this kind of way. She feels that the local vicar is quite out of touch with current educational thinking and that he is not really competent to teach or to take assemblies in the school. Although he does not seem to take a great deal of interest in the life of the school, she rather wishes that he would take even less interest. In short, she says that by coming into schools clergy often do more harm than good.

Susan's ideas on teaching tend to favour the modern or progressive approach to primary education. She believes in an informal classroom environment, where children are allowed to move freely around the classroom and to talk with one another about their work and interests. She does not mind children wandering in and out of her classroom without seeking permission to do so. She generally likes to follow a project approach to learning which adopts a totally integrated understanding of the various subjects, rather than following a timetable for different lessons.

Susan comes out very strongly against what she regards as old fashioned teaching methods, like the rote learning of multiplication tables and the frequent use of spelling tests or maths tests. She does not believe in giving stars or other credits for good work. She does not believe in the idea of streaming according to ability. She rates free expression much more highly than neat writing and correct punctuation. Behind this informal approach to education, Susan believes that it is important to maintain a firm control and discipline and she believes in taking a firm line with individual pupils who persistently disrupt the class. Susan is quite clear that none of these decisions about how to teach should be made differently in the case of church schools from county schools.

Susan believes that the school should be equally concerned with the pupils' intellectual and personal development. She believes that it is just as important to promote enjoyment of school as to promote a high level of academic attainment. She believes that it is just as important to help the slower pupils as to bring out the best in the brighter pupils. She feels that teachers should be available to counsel individual children as well as to teach them. Again, she believes that these are features of school life which should be equally characteristic of county schools and church schools.

In her list of curriculum priorities, Susan gives an equal weight of importance to the majority of teaching subjects. She rates maths, english, sciences, moral education, sex education, art, social studies, physical education and environmental studies as all very important. The only two subjects which she places in a category of lower priority are music and religious education. She regards music as being of secondary importance in all primary schools; she regards religious education as being of secondary importance in church schools and of no importance at all today in county schools.

The kind of religious education which Susan envisages being appropriate in church schools is the phenomenological approach to the subject. She believes that the first objective of religious education should be to teach about world religions. She also believes that religious education should be integrated as far as possible with secular subjects. She does not believe that the job of church schools should be to teach their pupils about God, Jesus, the bible or church services.

Susan regards moral education as being of considerably more importance than religious education. For Susan, moral education is something quite independent of religious education; consequently, the moral education taught in church schools should be identical with the moral education taught in county schools. She sees the aim of moral education to be directed towards helping children to make their own responsible moral choices. She does not believe that the school should emphasise the importance of obeying rules, good manners, tidiness, and so on. Rather, moral education should be concerned with teaching children to accept others and to think for themselves.

The relationship between the school and the local community is an aspect of school life which Susan takes very seriously. She believes that the primary school teacher has the responsibility to know as much as possible about the individual pupils' home backgrounds, and to develop close contacts with their parents. She remains wary, however, of encouraging parents to become too closely involved in the life of the school, and she is far from convinced that the teacher's job should extend to being available to counsel individual parents when they come seeking advice or help. On the more general front, Susan believes that it is important to build up relationships between the school and the wider local community. However, as she understands the local community, the clergy play a very insignificant part in it. She is not in favour of even church schools developing close contacts with the local clergy, or of encouraging the clergy to visit the school regularly.

Susan feels very strongly that church schools should not set out to present their pupils with the atmosphere of a Christian community. She believes that it is totally irrelevant to the function of the school whether the teachers are Christians or not. She believes that it is inappropriate for teachers in church schools to say classroom prayers, and that it should not be an important feature of the life of the school to provide a regular Christian assembly. She argues that it is totally inappropriate for church schools to have a school communion service or to accept responsibility for preparing pupils for confirmation.

Thus, in Susan we meet one of the younger recruits to the teaching staff of church schools in the diocese. Susan's attitude towards the church school system is a very negative one. Although herself a member of the Church of England, Susan is convinced of the importance of keeping religious interests out of the classroom. The children whom she teaches will be educated just as if they were attending a totally secular county school. While maintaining the name of a church school in the parish of Woolstock, the local church must accept that the main influence exerted in Susan's class is very far from being church related.

Grace Goodenough

Grace Goodenough is coming to the close of her teaching career. She is now in her late fifties, and holds a scale one post in the Church of England voluntary controlled first school at Lower Fosfield, a three-teacher village school still housed in the building originally opened in the 1880s. Before transferring to Lower Fosfield school, Grace had taught only in county schools, and her clear preference would still be to work in a county school. She moved to Lower Fosfield when her former county school closed some fifteen years ago.

Grace admits that she does not really understand the church school system. She does not know what makes a church aided school different from a church controlled school, and she is not at all interested in finding out. She is convinced that Lower Fosfield is an aided school, although the school's controlled status is well advertised in the school's information brochure and on the school notice board.

As far as her own religious commitment is concerned, Grace regards herself as a member of the Church of England, and she usually attends an Anglican church for the major Christian festivals, like Christmas and Harvest. Since she does not live in Lower Fosfield, she never thinks of attending services in the church with which her school is associated.

Grace feels very strongly that there is no real future for church schools in today's society. She believes that the church school system has outlived its usefulness. She argues that there are still far too many church schools and that now they should be given over to the state. She reacts forcefully against the suggestion that the Church of England should try to strengthen its position in secondary education. She feels that part of the problem with church schools is their denominational distinctiveness: if church schools are to be kept, at least they should become interdenominational and not remain exclusively Anglican.

If church schools are to remain, not only does Grace feel that they should give up their denominational identity, she believes that they should operate in exactly the same way as county schools. She can see no justification for church schools trying to recruit staff on religious criteria. She argues that teachers need exactly the same initial training and qualifications for working in church schools as county schools. Nor does she consider that there is a case for providing special in-service training for teachers in church schools.

Similarly, Grace can see no justification for church schools trying to govern pupil admissions on religious criteria. She argues that church schools should admit every child from the neighbourhood, just like county schools. She does not believe that church schools should try to give priority to the children of church-going parents, or to children with special needs. She believes that it is fundamentally wrong for church-going parents to seek a special sort of school for their children.

In the kind of rural area in which she teaches, Grace is not aware of any social or racial problems caused by church schools. Her own school functions as a neighbourhood school and so does not in any way discriminate against racial minorities or the socially deprived. On the other hand, she does believe that rural church schools can be divisive among the teaching profession. She is convinced that Church of England schools give unfair advantages to Christian teachers in the promotion stakes. As far as their impact on the pupils is concerned, Grace feels that church schools tend to be counter-productive from the church's point of view: she reckons that Church of England schools often alienate their pupils from the church.

Grace's negative attitude towards the church school system owes a lot more to her own set of experiences than to a well thought through philosophy of the relationship between education and religion. She is against church schools, but she is not against the idea of schools being an appropriate cradle for the Christian faith. She believes that it is educationally sound for schools not only to teach the Christian faith, but also to try to convert children to the Christian faith. She believes that it is equally appropriate for church schools and county schools to set out to initiate children into a religious faith. On this basis, she is in favour of schools taking on the characteristics of a believing or worshipping community, and of expecting pupils to engage in acts of worship during assembly time.

Similarly, Grace feels that it is an appropriate aim for religious education in county schools as well as in church schools to encourage pupils to accept and practise the Christian faith. Although she recognises that the home is often more important than the school in determining the child's religious commitment, she does not accept the idea that Christian education should be left to the pupils' homes or to the churches. Grace belongs firmly to the age of confessional RE. She is equally firmly committed to the notion that confessional RE should not be denominationally based.

The diocesan education office is a very remote institution as far as Grace is concerned. She feels that her school possibly has very little contact with the diocesan education office, but she would not wish it to be otherwise. She feels that neither she as an individual teacher, nor her school as a church foundation needs any particular help from the diocese.

Far from complaining that the local church does not take enough interest in Lower Fosfield school, Grace heartily wishes that the church would give less attention to the school and leave it well alone. She feels that the foundation governors have far too much contact with the school, and that they have far too much influence on what goes on. She resents this because she feels that the kind of involvement they have in the school is usually inappropriate and misinformed. She says very strongly that the foundation governors do not adequately understand the role of Church of England schools today.

While critical of foundation governors as a whole, Grace's real *bête noire* is the clergy. The local clergyman often comes into Lower Fosfield school, and she feels that he is a disaster. She says that he does more harm than good by coming into the school. She complains that the vicar is not aware of current educational thinking; he is not competent to teach; he is not competent to take assembly; he cannot keep order. She says that "sometimes he just writes on the board in atrocious writing and children have to sit and copy or try to copy". She concludes that "it all comes down to a clergyman needs teacher training if he is going to teach in a school". Without this professional competence, Grace says that it would be far better for the clergy to keep away from the school: "untrained clergy are useless".

Although in terms of age, Grace is one of the senior teachers in the church schools in the diocese, her overall approach to teaching is far from being old-fashioned or formal. Grace would clearly place herself among those who favour modern or progressive educational methods. She puts a high importance on encouraging self-expression. She believes in giving her pupils the freedom to talk to one another in class and to move around the teaching area. She does not insist on children seeking her permission before leaving the classroom. Her teaching day adopts an integrated approach to the different school subjects: she does not believe in following a timetable for different lessons.

Grace does not believe in many of the traditional goals of primary school teaching. She does not expect her pupils to learn their multiplication tables by heart. She does not believe in giving regular tests, or rewarding good work with stars or credit marks. She believes that it is much more important to encourage the pupils' creativity than to worry about spelling mistakes, grammatical errors or handwriting. She believes that informal educational methods work best when they are underpinned by a firm and reliable discipline, but she would never regard herself as a strict disciplinarian, and she tries not to let situations arise in which she would find it necessary to punish pupils.

Grace believes that the aim of the school should be to promote equally the pupils' personal development and their intellectual development. She argues that schools should both promote a high level of academic attainment and create a caring environment. She argues that teachers should both try to bring the best out of bright pupils and promote enjoyment of school among all pupils. She believes that teachers should be sensitive to the needs of individual pupils and be available to counsel those children in particular need.

In order to carry out this dual function most effectively, Grace believes that schools have a real responsibility to get to know the pupils' parents, to learn about their home background and to know as much as possible about the local community of which they are part. She reckons that teachers should give time to parents and be available to help them should they come seeking help.

Looking in detail at the curriculum of the first school, Grace wants to order the various subjects into three levels of priority. The highest level of priority Grace gives to maths, english, reading and moral education. The second level of priority she gives to science, music, social studies, religious education and environmental studies. The lowest level of priority is given to physical education, art and sex education.

As is consistent with her confessional, non-denominational approach to religious education, Grace says that the religious education she teaches gives most weight to teaching about God, Jesus and Christianity. In second place, she puts teaching about the bible and about the church. Her view of religious education does not involve teaching about church services or enabling children to take their place in the church community. She is adamant that religious education does not extend to include teaching about other world religions apart from Christianity. Grace's confessional approach to religious education includes the idea that religious education should be taught by committed Christians.

These traditional views on religious education sit uncomfortably alongside Grace's more modern views on education in general.

The notion of moral education which Grace has in mind holds in tension a blend of the old fashioned and the modern. She seems to want to inculcate in her pupils both a moral autonomy and a moral heteronomy. She believes in teaching children both to obey rules and to think morally for themselves.

Although Grace reacts very strongly against the church being involved in the maintenance of church schools, she feels equally strongly that all schools have a responsibility to be a Christian environment. She places a strong emphasis on schools providing an atmosphere of Christian community and on teachers publicly putting into practice Christian values. She remains strongly in favour of all schools providing a daily Christian assembly, involving a true act of worship. She also believes in encouraging the practice of saying classroom prayers. Her only caveat on the Christian involvement of schools is that the clergy should be kept at a good arm's length.

Grace is very firm that the fact that she now teaches in a church school has no bearing at all on her educational priorities and the decisions about how and what she teaches. She would be doing exactly the same in a county school. The provision of a church voluntary controlled school in Lower Fosfield is clearly making no difference to the children in Grace Goodenough's class.

Thus, in Grace we meet a teacher who is working in the church school system under sufferance. In particular, she has grown very bitter towards the local vicar and co-operates with him minimally. Faults probably exist on both sides, but neither of them seem in a position to help the other. In the instance of Lower Fosfield, the church school becomes a centre of conflict between education and the local church, not a point of reconciliation and constructive co-operation.

Judith Wright

Like Susan Hollings, Judith Wright is a young woman in her first teaching job after leaving college. Unlike Susan Hollings, Judith Wright is very much in favour of the church school system. She is teaching in St Philip's Church of England Voluntary Aided Primary School, one of the few church schools in the diocese which operates a selective admissions policy, giving priority to the children of church-going parents.

When she was looking for her first teaching post, Judith did not specifically seek a job in a church aided school, but she is very glad that such a post came her way. She is herself an active member of the Church of England and believes that church schools are an important way to develop links between children and the church. Although she does not live near her school, she travels in every Sunday to attend the main service at the parish church associated with the school.

The way in which St Philip's school is structured very much fits Judith's notions about the purposes of a church school. She believes that church schools should set out to provide a distinctive form of education for the children of church-going parents. She does not accept the philosophy that church schools should work in the same way as county schools by admitting every child from the neighbourhood. For this reason, Judith can see little point in the church holding on to its controlled schools. As far as she can see, the church should either convert controlled schools to become aided schools, or else hand them over totally to the state as county schools.

Judith feels that the present situation in which the church has many more primary school places than secondary school places is very silly. She would particularly like to see the church's large investment in primary controlled schools replaced with a few secondary aided schools. She also feels that what is important in today's society is the development of distinctive Christian schools rather than exclusively Anglican schools. For this reason, she would very much want to support the development of ecumenical schools.

If church schools are going to offer something really distinctive for the children of church-going parents, Judith feels that they should take great care in the way they recruit their staff. She strongly believes that only committed church people should be appointed to teach in Church of England schools and that teachers should receive special initial and in-service training to equip them for work in church schools. At present she is concerned that the Church of England does not take enough care in training and recruiting staff for church schools, with the consequence that church schools tend to lack qualified and effective Christian teachers. She argues that the Roman Catholic Church makes a much better job of running and staffing its church schools than the Church of England. Although a committed Anglican herself, Judith says that she would much rather be teaching in a Roman Catholic aided school than a Church of England aided school, because she reckons that the Roman Catholic schools operate on a much clearer philosophy about their identity and purpose.

Judith knows that if church schools are going to operate a distinctive admissions policy and provide a separate system for the children of church- going parents, these schools will have to face up to criticisms about being socially and racially divisive. She does not dismiss this problem at all lightly, but feels that, as things are in Suffolk, these are not insurmountable objections to the church school system. Christian parents, she argues, surely have a right to provide a Christian education for their children.

She also recognises that church schools can be accused of alienating children against religion, rather than promoting their positive religious development. When this is the case, she feels that the individual schools are to blame rather than the church school system itself. Certainly, she feels that St Philip's school makes an important and positive contribution to the pupils' religious faith.

When pressed to consider the differences between church schools and county schools, Judith answers almost exclusively in terms of the kind of religious education given and the kind of Christian community expressed by the school. She does not feel that the differences should extend to influence other areas of curriculum or to determine the kind of teaching methods used in the school.

As a teacher, Judith rather favours traditional teaching methods. She believes in adopting a strict discipline and in expecting pupils to seek permission before moving around or leaving the classroom. She believes in the practice of giving regular spelling tests and regular maths tests. What is particularly interesting is the way in which she argues that these educational goals should apply equally in church schools and county schools. The fact that she is teaching in a church school makes no difference to the way in which she organises her classroom.

As far as the content of the curriculum is concerned, Judith believes that equal weight should be given to subjects like art and music, environmental and social studies, religious education and moral education, as to maths, reading and writing. Judith argues for a balanced curriculum which gives the pupils a wide perspective on learning. The only curriculum area which she is willing to relegate to an inferior status is physical education. She feels that physical education and games are best left for outside school hours. Again, Judith's decisions about the curriculum are not affected by the fact that she teaches in a church school.

Judith does not draw a close link between religious education and moral education. Her image of moral development involves a balanced blend between moral autonomy and heteronomy. She argues that

147

children should be taught to obey rules, but at the same time they should be trained in self discipline and to think for themselves.

Similarly, Judith does not believe that the church-related nature of a school should make a great difference to the school's attitude towards the pupils. She argues that all schools, church and county schools alike, should do all they can to create a caring environment, to promote the pupils' enjoyment of school and to develop the pupils' confidence in the staff. All schools should show that every pupil is respected, irrespective of ability or appearance. All schools should give equal weight to helping the slower pupils and to bringing the best out of the brighter pupils. All schools should take seriously the total development of their pupils and be available to counsel and help them on personal issues as well as academic matters.

Judith does not place a high level of importance on the school developing close contacts with the pupils' homes or with the local community, apart from through the church. She does not feel that it is particularly important for the teachers to know a great deal about the pupils' home backgrounds, nor does she want particularly to encourage parents to help in the school. She does not feel that church schools have any more responsibility to work alongside or to help individual parents than county schools.

The only link between the local community and the school which Judith feels is worth developing concerns the link with the local churches, and this is a link which she feels is specifically the prerogative of the church school. Church schools, she argues, should develop particularly close contact with the clergy and encourage the clergy to make regular visits to the school.

While she believes in the theory that there should be close contacts between church schools and the clergy, Judith's experience of this theory in practice has been far from encouraging. It seems that St Philip's school has quite a lot of contact with the clergy and at times Judith feels that this tends to do more harm than good to the development of positive relationships between the pupils and the local church. Judith likes some of the assemblies which the vicar leads in the school, but she is much less confident about the way in which he takes religious education lessons. She feels that the clergy need proper training for their work in church schools and that so often this training is just not given.

Nevertheless, Judith appreciates the effort which the vicar makes to have contact with the church school in his parish. As chairman of the governors, he is often seen around the school; the staff know him and talk with him. If it were not for the vicar's personal interest in the school, the contact with the local church would be very weak. The other foundation governors seem to take very little active interest in the life of the school. Similarly, the parochial church council and the church congregation seem hardly aware of the importance of having a church aided school so closely attached to their church.

Judith feels that the diocese should be doing more to help foster links between church schools and the local church. Perhaps the diocese should be more involved in training clergy and governors for their work in church schools. Perhaps the diocese should give a better lead in developing curriculum materials which the clergy could use in their church schools. Perhaps the diocesan education office could have more direct contact with individual schools and help them to develop and to assess their work.

Judith would like to see a greater link between the religious education given in the school and the life of the local church. She believes that this is one of the key ways in which church schools can offer something quite distinctive to their pupils. She does not believe that it is enough for religious education in the church school to teach simply about God, Jesus and the bible. She believes that the church school should also be giving special attention to teaching about the church and to introducing pupils to the worship of the church.

At the same time, Judith is quite adamant that church schools should not be taking time to teach their pupils about other world faiths. According to Judith, the job of the church school is to work alongside parents and the churches to encourage pupils to accept and to practise the Christian faith. For Judith, this is what makes the aims of religious education in Church of England schools so different from those in county schools.

As part of her belief that church schools should be different from county schools, Judith argues that there is a greater place for worship in the church school. She feels that it is important for church schools to hold a daily Christian assembly and to conduct classroom prayers. She feels that it is appropriate for church schools to celebrate the occasional communion service in school and, indeed, to help to prepare pupils for confirmation. Against this background, Judith believes that it is possible to speak about a specifically Christian view of education. The two keys to this specifically Christian view of education are confessional religious education and a Christian environment.

The Christian environment which Judith envisages as being characteristic of the church school, she reckons is made possible by having a number of committed Christian teachers on the staff. It is through these committed teachers that church schools can become places where Christian values are daily put into practice.

Thus, in Judith we meet a young Christian teacher who very much wants to apply her faith as a teacher working in a distinctive type of ecumenical church school. Since her present post is not allowing her to develop this ideal as fully as she would like, she has begun to wonder whether she might be better suited in a different type of school. Her sights are now set on trying to find a post in a Roman Catholic aided primary school. While this would not allow her to fulfil her vision of working in an ecumenical context, she feels that it would help her to fulfil more adequately her vocation as a Christian teacher committed to developing links between church and school.

Philip Wilding

Philip Wilding holds a scale two post in St Margaret's Middle School at Freshlake, one of the four Church of England voluntary controlled middle schools opened in the diocese during the 1970s. Before moving to St Margaret's School, Philip had taught only in county schools.

Philip is in his early thirties, and he regards himself as a humanist. He shares no Christian beliefs and he never attends church. He has no particular desire to teach in a church school, but does not mind doing so either. He says that he has no real preference regarding the type of school in which he teaches. He applied for his present post because it carried promotion to a scale two salary and the associated responsibilities.

Although Philip is not in any sense enthusiastic about teaching in a church school, neither is he particularly critical of the church school system. He does not feel that the church school system has outlived its usefulness, nor does he feel that the Church of England should reduce the number of schools with which it is associated.

If there were to be changes in the current system of church schools, Philip would advocate two changes. First, he considers that there is more justification for the church to maintain controlled schools than aided schools: he recommends that the churches should give up their claim to aided schools. Second, he considers that there is more justification in today's society for the maintenance of ecumenical church schools, rather than strictly denominational schools: he recommends that the Church of England should try to co-operate more with the other churches.

The kind of church school system which Philip favours is one which does not draw any sharp distinctions between church schools and county schools. It is for this reason that he favours the controlled status rather than the aided status. To begin with, Philip does not believe that church schools should seek to appoint a different kind of teacher from county schools. He does not believe that church schools should give preference to appointing committed Christians to teaching posts, nor seek out those who have received any form of special initial or in-service training to equip them for work in church schools.

Second, Philip does not believe that church schools should seek to adopt a radically different kind of admissions policy from county schools. He argues that the first priority of church schools should be to admit every child from the neighbourhood, just like county schools; but, then, he concedes that church schools should have a secondary priority of also admitting the children of church-going parents from a wider geographical area.

Philip does not accept that many of the criticisms usually levelled against church schools are really justified in his own experience. He has found no evidence to support the contentions that church schools give unfair privileges to some pupils; that they are racially or socially divisive; or that they give unfair advantages to Christian teachers in the promotion stakes. However, he does believe that there are grounds to suspect that church schools are far from helpful to the church's own work. He reckons that church schools often help to turn pupils away from Christianity and from the church.

Philip believes that a clear distinction needs to be made between the task which it is appropriate for the churches to undertake and the task which it is appropriate for schools to undertake. Philip belongs to a generation of teachers which has begun to differentiate clearly between religion and education. He argues quite firmly that it is neither the task of county schools nor church schools to attempt to initiate children into a religious faith. He considers that it is educationally unsound for Church of England schools to try to teach the Christian faith or to try to convert children to the Christian faith. He believes that in today's society it is no longer appropriate to ask children to worship God in school assembly.

The kind of religious education which Philip envisages as appropriate within his school has as its main aim helping children understand what religion is and what it would mean to take a religion seriously. According to Philip, the primary purpose of religious education is to teach children about religion, not to teach children to be religious. Even in church schools he feels that it is inappropriate for religious education to have a denominational component. For example, he reacts very strongly against the suggestion that church schools should teach their pupils about the communion service or that they should have the communion celebrated in school. Philip wants to place the real task of religious education firmly in the hands of parents and the churches, not in the hands of teachers and schools.

Philip feels that it is possible to teach in St Margaret's School without being all that conscious of the fact that it is a church school. He has little idea about the actual or potential contacts that go on between the school and the church. He does not know the foundation governors of the school, so he is in no position to comment on the value of the contribution which they make to the life of the school. He has no particular interest in the diocesan education office either. He does not know whether the diocese has much contact with the school or not.

The one way in which St Margaret's stands out in Philip's mind as a church school is that the local clergy are sometimes seen in the school. The clergy do not come to school that often, but Philip believes that they certainly make their presence felt on the occasions when they do visit the school. From the church's point of view, Philip reckons that the clergy's visits do more harm than good. The clergy's main reason for coming into St Margaret's School seems to be to take assemblies. Philip often finds their assemblies to be most embarrassing. He feels that the clergy are not properly trained for working among children of the age who attend St Margaret's School, and because they are not properly trained they make a bad job of it.

Philip's approach to teaching in a middle school is based on his training as a secondary school teacher. He believes that it is much more appropriate to treat middle school pupils like secondary pupils, rather than like primary pupils. He believes in the school adopting a firm framework of discipline, but not a strict or repressive discipline. He does not believe in the informal environment of the primary school. By the time they reach the middle school, he believes that children should be ready to accept a regular timetable and a more formal teaching environment.

As far as the curriculum is concerned, Philip believes that the most weight should be given to maths, english and the sciences. He puts everything else in second place, including music, art, social studies, physical education, environmental studies, religious education, moral education and sex education. He argues that the priority given to all these subjects, including religious education, should be exactly the same in church schools as in county schools.

Philip's theory about the function of religious education argues that exactly the same weight should be given to the other world religions as to Christianity. His approach to teaching Christianity emphasises the objective nature of religious studies. Even in church schools, he considers that it is inappropriate for religious education to include teaching about church services. He does not believe that religious education needs to be taught by those who are themselves committed Christian believers.

Philip's theory about the function of moral education argues that the first goal of the school should be to teach children to think for themselves, rather than to do as they are told. He believes that it is important to teach children to accept others. He does not believe that schools should be concerned to teach children to obey rules, to be tidy and so on. Again, he argues that the kind of moral education given in church schools should be exactly the same as that which is appropriate within county schools.

Philip believes quite firmly that it is a mistake to try to think of the church school as an extension of the church itself, or as a special kind of Christian community. He does not accept that it is part of the job of the school to prepare pupils for confirmation. He does not support having regular Christian assemblies, or classroom prayers. As a humanist, Philip does not believe that schools should be trying to put Christian values into practice or to provide an atmosphere of a Christian community. He believes that in today's society schools should be trying to cut all these ties to the Christian past.

According to Philip it is the job of schools to create a caring environment, but this should happen on educational grounds, not on religious grounds. Philip believes that it is very important for schools to demonstrate that they respect each pupil irrespective of ability or appearance. He places a higher priority on helping the slower pupils and those who have personal problems, than on promoting the academic attainment of the brighter pupils. He believes that it is very important that children should enjoy their time at school, and that they should have a lot of confidence in the staff.

Working in a middle school which draws children from a number of rural communities, Philip argues that it is often very difficult to build up contacts with the pupils' parents and to know much about their individual home backgrounds. He believes that a school should try to build up relationships with parents as much as possible, but then also to accept the fact that in many cases this is unlikely to happen. He reckons that the clergy can be one way of developing contacts between the school and the many communities it serves, but so far his experiences of the clergy do not encourage him to pursue this line.

When the diocese was considering the case for the church's involvement in middle schools in the late 1960s, it stressed the importance of maintaining the church's contact with this age group of children. Certainly as far as Philip Wilding is concerned, it is not part of his intention as a teacher in one of these new controlled middle schools to further the church's hopes in this direction.

10 DISCUSSION

This study has set out to organise an account of the historical development and contemporary interpretation of the place of Church of England rural primary schools within the state maintained sector. The historical account has documented the consistent erosion of the church's contribution to rural primary education, while current financial pressures on local education authorities to close small schools indicate the likely acceleration of this process. The contemporary account of the attitudes and views of those who currently teach in the church schools has documented the lack of consensus among teachers as to their precise role within the church voluntary sector of rural primary education.

If the vision of a partnership between church and state in rural primary education is to have any clear meaning or practical cutting edge towards the end of the twentieth century, the Church of England needs to think clearly about its aims and objectives in the provision of school sites and about its commitment to those who staff church schools. Given the nature of the Church of England, these are issues which need to be tackled as thoroughly at the local levels of school governing bodies and parochial church councils as at diocesan and national levels.

With this end in mind, instead of finishing with a summary of my own conclusions, I have organised a list of the key questions raised in my mind by the earlier chapters which discuss in detail the views of those who teach in church schools. In sequencing these questions I have deliberately placed the key issues raised by chapter one at the end of the sequence so that they can be faced in the light of reflection on the empirical data provided by the research project. I hope that this final section will become one of the vehicles through which local churches and local school governing bodies, as well as diocesan education committees, will be able to assess their own work through church schools and their commitment to the teachers who staff these schools.

Chapter 4 The teachers

1   Are church schools 'equal opportunity employers', giving equal chances of promotion to men and women?

2 Do church schools give better promotional opportunities to church-going members of the Church of England and should they do so?

3 Should church schools be trying to recruit staff who particularly want to teach in the voluntary sector?

Chapter 5 Attitudes to church schools

4 Should any form of special initial training be available for those who want to teach in church schools?

5 What kind of in-service training should be available for teachers in church schools?

6 What kind of admissions policy should church schools operate?

7 Is there a future for church schools and, if so, is this most likely as denominational or interdenominational schools?

8 Has the Church of England been wise to concentrate its resources in primary education rather than secondary?

9 Are church schools racially or socially divisive?

10 Are education and catechesis contradictory or complementary?

11 Is it possible to speak of a distinctively Christian view of education?

12 Should religious education in the church school be the same as religious education in the county school?

13 Should the diocese have greater responsibility for individual church schools?

14 What kind of relationship should exist between a church school and the local church?

15 Is adequate care taken in appointing and training foundation governors for church schools?

16 Are clergy adequately equipped for their work with church schools?

Chapter 6 Attitudes to teaching

17 What priority should be given to religious education in a church school?

18 How is religious education best taught in a church school?

19 To what extent should church schools emphasise Christian values?

20 Is there a place for the communion to be celebrated in church schools?

21 What kind of 'school ethos' should be promoted in a church school?
22 What kind of relationship should exist between the church school and the local community?
23 In what way should parents be involved in the life of the church school?
24 In what way should clergy be involved in the life of the church school?
25 What kind of moral education should be given in the church school?
26 What are the advantages and disadvantages of the progressive and traditional methods of teaching in the church school?

Chapter 7 Ideas of distinctiveness

27 Is it right for church schools to give more emphasis to religious education and moral education than county schools?
28 What emphasis should be placed on sex education in the church school?
29 Should church schools be integrating religious education with secular subjects?
30 Should church schools be giving attention to the teaching of world religions?
31 Should church schools expect pupils to take part in Christian assemblies?
32 Should church schools aim to have religious education taught by committed Christians?
33 Should church schools be preparing pupils for confirmation?
34 Should church schools promote a different kind of 'school ethos' from county schools?
35 Should church schools have closer links with parents and the local community than county schools?
36 Should clergy have a different place in church schools than in county schools?
37 Should church schools have anything distinctive to contribute to moral education?
38 Should church schools have anything distinctive to contribute to the debate between progressive and traditional educational methods?

Chapter 8 Attitude formation

39 If teachers who do not attend church are less in favour of the church school system and if the younger generation of teachers are less inclined to attend church, what are the long term implications for attitudes towards church schools?

40 If the younger teachers are less inclined to emphasise the distinctiveness of church schools, what are the long term implications for the distinctive characteristics of church schools?

Chapter 1 Introduction

41 How strong are the arguments of the British Humanist Association and the Socialist Education Association against the church school system?

42 Is it more important to promote racial and social integration than to preserve the identity of minority groups, like Moslems and Christians, in a secular society?

43 What should the church's response be to the closure of small schools?

44 Are church schools the appropriate medium through which to promote the church's 'domestic' concern in education?

45 Is it appropriate for the church to maintain a 'general' concern in education when society is as secular as it is today?

46 Is it appropriate for the church to see the future of partnership in education in terms of voluntarism rather than denominationalism?

STATISTICAL APPENDIX

My aim in preparing this book has been to include the statistical information in the text itself and so to avoid frequent cross-referencing between tables and text. At the same time, it is helpful to provide an easy summary of the main statistics on which the text is based. The following tables are numbered in chapter sequence to facilitate cross-referencing with the text if the reader should so desire. In using these tables it needs to be remembered that the percentages have been rounded to the nearest whole numbers. This means that some rows will add up to 99 or 101; it also means that occasionally the aggregated figures reported in the text may differ from those aggregated figures which can be computed from the tables by one percentage point.

Partnership in Rural Education

2.1 Church schools closed or transferred since 1915

School	Year	School	Year
Braiseworth	1919	Groton	1934
Easton	1919	Rede	1934
Elmswell	1919	Wickham Market	1934
Denham (Eye)	1920	Little Whelnetham	1935
Helmingham	1920	Shottisham	1935
Ringshall	1920	Stanningfield	1935
Rushmere St Andrew	1920	Alpheton	1936
Denham (Bury St Edmunds)	1921	South Elmham St Cross	1936
Horham	1921	Ampton	1937
Little Cornard	1921	Bury St Eds St James Boys	1937
Theberton	1921	Bury St Eds St James Girls	1937
Uggeshall	1921	Bury St Eds St James Infants	1937
Aldeburgh	1922	South Elmham St James	1937
Aspall	1922	Syleham	1937
Bromeswell	1922	Boyton	1938
Knodishall	1922	Ipswich St Helen	1938
Langham	1922	Newton Green	1938
Layham	1922	Beccles	1939
West Stow	1922	Mendlesham	1939
Westhall	1922	Dallinghoo	1941
Halesworth	1923	Wrentham	1943
Lackford	1923	Yaxley	1943
Sutton	1923	Great Bricett	1944
Winston	1923	Ilketshall St Margaret	1944
Burgate	1924	Culford Heath	1946
Cransford	1924	Felsham	1947
Stratford St Andrew	1924	Great Saxham	1947
Monewden	1925	Hawstead	1947
Brent Eleigh	1927	Herringswell	1947
Chelsworth	1927	Kentford	1947
Lindsey	1927	Monk Soham	1947
Sapiston	1927	Preston	1947
Cavenham	1929	Stanstead	1947
Fakenham Magna	1929	Tostock	1947
Ipswich St Peter	1930	Troston	1947
Badingham	1931	Wattisham	1947
Witnesham	1931	Bedingfield	1948
Southwold	1932	Chillesford	1948
Holbrook	1933	Hargrave	1948
Ipswich St Mary Stoke	1933	Heveningham	1948
Brantham	1934	Bradfield Combust	1949
Brantham Cattawade	1934	Kenton	1949

2.1 **Church schools closed or transferred since 1915** (continued)

School	Year	School	Year
Leavenheath	1949	Wyverstone	1963
Little Saxham	1949	Cotton	1964
Thorpe Morieux	1949	Offton	1964
Bradfield St Clare	1950	Weybread	1964
Debach	1950	Ilketshall St Andrew	1965
Iken	1950	Saxstead	1965
Sudbourne	1950	Wherstead	1965
Long Melford St Catherine	1951	Onehouse	1966
Fornham St Martin	1952	Barham	1967
Mickfield	1953	Great Bradley	1967
Thornham Magna	1953	Great Thurlow	1967
Thrandeston	1953	Hawkedon	1967
Thelnetham	1955	South Elmham All Saints	1967
Euston	1956	Stowlangtoft	1967
Hasketon	1956	Flempton	1968
Hessett	1957	Freston	1968
Rendlesham	1957	Kedington	1968
Burstall	1958	Metfield	1968
Worlington	1958	Baylham	1969
Brettenham	1959	Brome and Oakley	1969
Dalham	1959	Hitcham	1969
Hinderclay	1959	Ashfield Magna	1970
Poslingford	1959	Coddenham	1970
Coney Weston	1960	Freckenham	1970
Denston	1960	Wingfield	1970
Edwardstone	1960	Earl Stonham	1971
Hacheston	1960	Eriswell	1971
Great Livermere	1960	Harkstead	1971
Market Weston	1960	Sotterley	1971
Nowton	1960	Bury St Edmunds St John	1972
Withersfield	1960	Bury St Edmunds St Mary	1972
Crowfield	1961	Frostenden	1972
Huntingfield	1961	Great Glemham	1972
Blaxhall	1962	Ousden	1972
Cratfield	1962	Bury St Edmunds Victoria St	1973
Henstead	1962	Butley	1973
Higham	1962	Sibton	1973
Barsham	1963	Woolverstone	1973
Dunwich	1963	Alderton	1974
Little Glemham	1963	Campsea Ash	1974
		Tunstall	1974

2.2 Church schools established before the formation of the diocese in 1915 and maintained in January 1984 as controlled schools

School	School
Acton	Hartest
Bardwell	Haughley
Barnham	Hepworth
Barningham	Hintlesham and Chattisham
Barrow	Honington and Sapiston
Bawdsey	Hopton
Bedfield	Horringer
Benhall	Ingham
Bentley	Ixworth
Boxford	Kelsale
Bradfield St George	Kersey
Bramfield National	Lawshall
Bramford	Little Thurlow
Brampton	Long Melford
Bures St Marys	Mellis
Bury St Edmunds Eastgate St	Monks Eleigh
Capel St Mary	Moulton
Cavendish	Nacton
Charsfield	Norton
Chedburgh	Old Newton
Chelmondiston	Pakenham
Chevington	Palgrave
Cockfield	Rattlesden
Cookley and Walpole	Redgrave
Culford	Rickinghall
Dennington	Ringsfield
Drinkstone	Risby
East Bergholt	Rougham
Elmsett	Shimpling
Eyke	Sproughton
Finningham	Stoke by Clare
Flixton	Stoke by Nayland
Fressingfield	Stradbroke
Gazeley	Stutton
Gislingham	Sudbury St Peter and St Gregory
Great Barton	Sudbury Tudor
Great Finborough	Tattingstone
Great Waldingfield	Thorndon All Saints
Great Whelnetham	Thurston

2.2 Church schools established before the formation of the diocese in 1915 and maintained in January 1984 as controlled schools (continued)

School	School
Tuddenham St Mary	Wetheringsett
Walsham le Willows	Whatfield
Wattisfield	Wilby
Wetherden	Worlingham
	Worlingworth

2.3 Church schools established before the formation of the diocese in 1915 and maintained in January 1984 as aided schools

School	School
Badwell Ash	Ipswich St Margaret
Creeting St Mary	Ipswich St Matthew
Debenham Sir Robert Hitcham	Laxfield All Saints
Elveden	Mildenhall
Eye St Peter and St Paul	Newmarket All Saints
Framlingham	Orford
Hadleigh St Mary	Parham
Icklingham	Stonham Aspal
Ipswich St John	Woodbridge St Mary

Partnership in Rural Education

2.4 Pupils in maintained primary and secondary schools for the county of Suffolk

January	All schools	County	Anglican controlled	Anglican aided	Roman Catholic
1967	69974	56456	8119	4166	1230
1968					
1969	75554	61448	8415	3839	1852
1970	78745	64245	8649	3873	1969
1971	81882	66818	8778	3900	2386
1972	85433	69907	9098	3819	2609
1973	87542	71239	9501	3991	2811
1974	94612	76917	11022	3795	2878
1975	95063	77840	10537	3731	2955
1976	97005	79512	10763	3742	2988
1977	98156	80544	11147	3498	2967
1978	100892	83302	11146	3445	2999
1979	101269	84232	10611	3351	3075
1980	100603	83749	10482	3337	3035
1981	98933	82360	10277	3265	3031
1982	97172	81018	9891	3223	3040
1983	95195	79414	9660	3117	3005
1984	93588	78037	9502	3092	2956

Note

Part-time pupils are counted as .5 full-time pupils

5.1 Teachers

	Controlled			Aided		
	A%	NC%	D%	A%	NC%	D%
I applied for my present post specifically because it was in a C of E school	10	6	84	37	5	58
I would not have applied for my present post had it been in a county school	2	5	94	13	12	75
Only committed church people should be appointed to teach in C of E schools	16	14	70	40	11	49
Teachers should receive special initial training for work in C of E schools	17	17	66	35	17	48
Teachers should receive special in-service training for work in C of E schools	25	20	55	42	19	39
There is a lack of qualified and effective teachers of religion in C of E schools	40	35	25	39	38	24

5.2 Admissions policy

	Controlled			Aided		
	A%	NC%	D%	A%	NC%	D%
C of E schools should only admit children of practising Anglicans	3	5	92	13	3	84
C of E schools should mainly admit children of church-going parents	6	6	88	32	6	62
Anglican parents should be encouraged to send their children to a C of E school	42	24	34	63	17	20
Church schools should admit every child from the neighbourhood just like county schools	88	7	5	57	10	33
C of E schools should give priority to children with special needs	21	26	53	32	21	47

Key   A   agree
          NC   not certain
          D   disagree

5.3 Future direction

	Controlled			Aided		
	A%	NC%	D%	A%	NC%	D%
The C of E has too many schools	12	42	45	8	26	65
The C of E school system has outlived its usefulness	16	24	60	10	10	80
C of E schools should be given over to the state	14	23	63	12	6	82
The C of E spends too much money on church schools	2	53	45	2	30	68
The Roman Catholic church makes a better job of running church schools than the C of E	24	50	25	19	55	26
The C of E should develop more secondary/middle/upper schools	33	38	29	60	20	21
I would support the development of inter-denominational church schools	66	23	11	74	16	10

5.4 Criticisms

	Controlled			Aided		
	A%	NC%	D%	A%	NC%	D%
C of E schools often alienate their pupils from the church	11	27	62	13	26	61
C of E schools often help to turn pupils away from Christianity	11	28	61	10	29	60
C of E schools are socially divisive	7	19	74	7	17	76
C of E schools are racially divisive	7	27	66	6	18	76
C of E schools give unfair privileges to some children	4	14	82	8	9	83
C of E schools give unfair advantages to Christian teachers in the promotion stakes	16	38	47	20	32	48

5.5 Commitment

	Controlled			Aided		
	A%	NC%	D%	A%	NC%	D%
It is not the task of county schools to initiate children into a religious faith	68	9	23	61	15	24
It is not the task of C of E schools to initiate children into a religious faith	58	12	30	36	8	55
There is no such thing as a specifically Christian view of education	33	14	53	24	9	66
The idea of 'worshipping God' in school assembly should be abandoned	15	13	72	3	2	95
It is inappropriate to mix education and evangelism	36	22	42	30	15	56
It is educationally unsound for C of E schools to try to teach the Christian faith	15	15	70	5	5	91
It is educationally unsound for C of E schools to try to convert children to the Christian faith	66	16	18	43	18	39

5.6 Religious education

	Controlled			Aided		
	A%	NC%	D%	A%	NC%	D%
The aims of RE in a C of E school should be the same as those in a county school	66	12	22	39	10	51
RE should help children to understand what religion is and what it would mean to take a religion seriously	89	5	6	92	3	6
Good RE should not involve denominational teaching	78	10	13	64	7	29
C of E schools should encourage pupils to accept and practise the Christian faith	66	13	21	88	6	6
C of E schools should teach their pupils about the communion service	35	27	38	66	14	20
C of E schools should have communion celebrated in school	6	16	78	23	19	58
Christian education is the job of parents and the church, not schools	20	8	72	10	7	83
Home is more important than school in determining the child's religious commitment	90	6	4	83	9	8

5.7 Diocese

	Controlled			Aided		
	A%	NC%	D%	A%	NC%	D%
The diocese should foster links between C of E schools and local churches	72	20	8	92	6	3
C of E schools are reluctant to accept help from the diocese in teaching RE	7	42	51	11	27	62
The C of E does not take enough interest in church schools	26	40	34	33	27	40
The diocese does not give enough help to C of E schools in teaching RE	36	37	27	38	27	35
Our school does not have enough contact with the diocesan education office	27	42	31	24	36	39
C of E schools need better teaching materials for RE than at present	58	18	25	61	12	27

5.8 Local church

	Controlled			Aided		
	A%	NC%	D%	A%	NC%	D%
Often foundation governors do not take enough interest in C of E schools	30	46	24	45	37	18
Teachers do not generally have enough contact with the foundation governors of C of E schools	49	26	25	64	22	14
Generally foundation governors take an active part in C of E schools	23	46	31	23	35	42
Foundation governors do not adequately understand the role of C of E schools today	32	49	19	41	46	13
Often local churches do not take enough interest in C of E schools	31	43	26	48	30	22
Our school does not have enough contact with the local church	16	10	74	20	8	72
Our school does not have enough contact with the clergy	17	10	73	26	7	67

5.9 Clergy

	Controlled			Aided		
	A%	NC%	D%	A%	NC%	D%
By coming into schools clergy often do more harm than good	15	22	63	12	16	72
Clergy are not generally competent to teach in C of E schools	39	35	27	35	34	31
Clergy are not generally competent to lead assemblies in school	28	25	47	21	27	52
Clergy do not seem to be adequately trained for involvement in C of E schools	59	33	9	64	24	12
Clergy are not generally aware of current educational thinking	44	38	18	50	33	17
When clergy teach RE in C of E schools they should follow the syllabus	52	16	32	54	18	29
Often clergy do not take enough interest in church schools	33	38	29	57	22	21
Clergy make good Governors for C of E schools	39	50	11	41	41	18

6.1 Curriculum

	Controlled			Aided		
	I%	U%	NA%	I%	U%	NA%
Teaching maths (numeracy)	98	1	1	100	0	0
Teaching english (literacy)	98	1	1	100	0	0
Teaching children to read	98	0	2	100	0	0
Teaching science	95	2	3	99	1	0
Teaching moral education	97	1	2	97	2	1
Teaching sex education	50	26	24	44	30	26
Teaching music	94	3	3	93	5	2
Teaching art	95	3	2	92	7	1
Teaching social studies	81	9	10	88	8	5
Teaching RE	91	7	2	98	0	2
Teaching PE	93	6	1	89	9	2
Teaching environmental studies	95	2	3	97	2	1

6.2 Religious education

	Controlled			Aided		
	I%	U%	NA%	I%	U%	NA%
Teaching about world religions	72	19	10	74	17	9
Teaching about Christianity	88	10	2	95	3	2
Teaching about Jesus	87	8	5	95	4	1
Teaching about God	86	9	5	96	2	2
Teaching about the bible	84	14	2	93	5	2
Teaching about the church	72	21	7	87	10	3
Teaching about church services	44	38	18	74	23	3
Integrating religious and secular studies	77	16	7	89	7	4

Key   I   regarded as important
          U   regarded as unimportant
          NA regarded as not applicable

6.3 Christian community

	Controlled			Aided		
	I%	U%	NA%	I%	U%	NA%
Providing a regular Christian assembly	83	14	4	94	4	2
Providing a daily Christian assembly	76	20	4	88	9	3
Saying classroom prayers	48	36	15	74	21	5
Preparing pupils for confirmation	10	31	60	27	33	40
Having a regular communion service for the school	6	35	59	22	35	43
Providing an atmosphere of Christian community	86	10	4	96	3	1
Having committed Christians on the staff	55	34	12	73	21	6
Having RE taught by a committed Christian	65	30	5	79	17	5
Putting into practise Christian values	94	3	3	99	0	1

6.4 School ethos

	Controlled			Aided		
	I%	U%	NA%	I%	U%	NA%
Creating a caring environment	99	0	1	100	0	0
Being available to counsel individual children	99	0	1	100	0	0
Respecting each pupil irrespective of ability or appearance	99	0	0	98	2	0
Promoting a high level of academic attainment	92	4	4	92	7	1
Helping the slower pupils	98	1	1	100	0	0
Bringing the best out of bright pupils	98	0	2	99	1	0
Promoting enjoyment of school	98	1	1	98	1	1
Promoting the pupils' confidence in the staff	98	1	1	100	0	0

6.5 Local community

	Controlled			Aided		
	I%	U%	NA%	I%	U%	NA%
Knowing about the pupils' home background	95	4	1	97	3	0
Developing a close contact with the local community	97	2	1	98	1	1
Developing close contacts with parents	99	0	0	98	2	0
Developing close contacts with clergy	64	28	8	78	21	1
Encouraging regular visits from clergy	70	23	7	83	15	2
Encouraging parents to help in the school	87	9	4	85	13	2
Being available to counsel individual parents	96	3	1	96	3	1

6.6 Images of the moral life

	Controlled			Aided		
	I%	U%	NA%	I%	U%	NA%
Teaching children good manners	96	3	1	100	0	0
Teaching children to be honest and truthful	99	0	0	99	1	0
Teaching children to live moral lives	94	2	4	95	0	5
Teaching children to obey rules	93	4	3	95	4	1
Training children in hard work	85	9	6	89	7	4
Teaching children to be tidy	88	9	3	93	6	1
Training children in self discipline	99	1	0	100	0	0
Training children to think for themselves	99	0	1	99	0	1
Teaching children to accept others	99	0	1	100	0	0
Training children to go to church regularly	24	38	38	47	32	21

6.7 Traditional methods

	Controlled			Aided		
	I%	U%	NA%	I%	U%	NA%
Adopting strict discipline	65	22	13	75	17	8
Adopting firm discipline	91	7	3	95	3	2
Streaming according to ability	28	40	32	38	40	23
Giving regular spelling tests	69	24	7	68	26	6
Giving regular maths tests	45	43	12	59	29	12
Following a regular timetable for different lessons	52	36	12	55	33	12
Correcting most spelling and grammatical errors	76	16	8	80	14	6
Giving stars or other credits for good work	54	35	11	59	30	10
Expecting children to seek permission before leaving the classroom	80	17	3	81	15	4
Punishing children for persistent disruptive behaviour	77	12	11	84	5	11
Teaching children to write clearly	95	2	3	98	2	0
Teaching children to know their multiplication tables by heart	75	18	7	77	17	6

6.8 Progressive methods

	Controlled			Aided		
	I%	U%	NA%	I%	U%	NA%
Adopting an integrated day	37	48	15	41	43	16
Encouraging self expression	96	2	1	96	4	0
Following a project approach to learning	70	25	5	62	31	7
Generally allowing children to talk to one another	83	13	4	83	11	6
Generally allowing children to decide where they sit	31	52	17	22	53	25
Generally allowing children to move around the classroom	65	29	6	62	31	7

Partnership in Rural Education

7.1 Curriculum

	Controlled			Aided		
	M%	S%	L%	M%	S%	L%
Teaching maths (numeracy)	6	93	0	6	94	0
Teaching english (literacy)	7	93	0	6	94	0
Teaching children to read	7	93	0	11	89	0
Teaching science	8	92	0	3	97	0
Teaching moral education	28	71	0	43	56	1
Teaching sex education	5	91	4	3	91	6
Teaching music	7	93	0	7	93	0
Teaching art	4	95	1	5	95	0
Teaching social studies	5	95	0	7	92	1
Teaching RE	48	51	2	65	34	1
Teaching PE	4	96	0	3	96	1
Teaching environmental studies	4	95	0	4	96	0

7.2 Religious education

	Controlled			Aided		
	M%	S%	L%	M%	S%	L%
Teaching about world religions	29	68	3	44	50	6
Teaching about Christianity	57	41	2	70	29	1
Teaching about Jesus	56	42	2	75	22	3
Teaching about God	54	44	2	74	25	1
Teaching about the bible	50	49	1	70	29	0
Teaching about the church	60	37	3	74	24	2
Teaching about church services	59	39	2	74	21	5
Integrating religious and secular studies	44	53	3	59	40	1

Key   M   more attention should be given in church schools
        S   the same attention should be given in church schools
        L   less attention should be given in church schools

7.3 Christian community

	Controlled			Aided		
	M%	S%	L%	M%	S%	L%
Providing a regular Christian assembly	49	50	1	63	36	1
Providing a daily Christian assembly	49	50	1	66	32	2
Saying classroom prayers	46	51	3	68	31	2
Preparing pupils for confirmation	39	57	5	59	37	4
Having a regular communion service for the school	29	64	7	47	45	8
Providing an atmosphere of Christian community	60	40	1	72	27	1
Having committed Christians on the staff	52	46	2	73	25	2
Having RE taught by a committed Christian	52	46	2	63	36	1
Putting into practise Christian values	52	48	0	79	20	1

7.4 School ethos

	Controlled			Aided		
	M%	S%	L%	M%	S%	L%
Creating a caring environment	20	80	0	52	48	0
Being available to counsel individual children	16	84	0	30	70	0
Respecting each pupil irrespective of ability or appearance	18	82	0	32	68	0
Promoting a high level of academic attainment	9	90	1	9	90	1
Helping the slower pupils	12	88	0	22	78	0
Bringing the best out of bright pupils	12	88	0	18	81	1
Promoting enjoyment of school	13	87	0	32	68	0
Promoting the pupils' confidence in the staff	8	92	0	24	75	1

7.5 Local community

	Controlled			Aided		
	M%	S%	L%	M%	S%	L%
Knowing about the pupils' home background	11	89	0	31	69	0
Developing a close contact with the local community	31	69	0	41	59	0
Developing close contacts with parents	17	83	0	29	71	0
Developing close contacts with clergy	63	35	2	81	18	1
Encouraging regular visits from clergy	64	33	3	78	20	2
Encouraging parents to help in the school	13	87	0	30	68	2
Being available to counsel individual parents	14	85	0	31	69	0

7.6 Images of the moral life

	Controlled			Aided		
	M%	S%	L%	M%	S%	L%
Teaching children good manners	17	83	0	30	70	0
Teaching children to be honest and truthful	19	80	1	36	64	0
Teaching children to live moral lives	24	76	0	41	59	0
Teaching children to obey rules	12	88	0	20	80	0
Training children in hard work	11	89	0	19	79	2
Teaching children to be tidy	8	91	0	15	85	0
Training children in self discipline	17	83	0	29	71	0
Training children to think for themselves	13	86	1	25	75	0
Teaching children to accept others	19	81	0	43	57	0
Training children to go to church regularly	40	57	3	62	36	2

7.7 Traditional methods

	Controlled			Aided		
	M%	S%	L%	M%	S%	L%
Adopting strict discipline	9	89	2	16	81	4
Adopting firm discipline	10	90	0	19	80	1
Streaming according to ability	5	88	7	7	83	10
Giving regular spelling tests	5	95	0	7	93	0
Giving regular maths tests	6	93	1	3	96	1
Following a regular timetable for different lessons	4	94	2	6	93	1
Correcting most spelling and grammatical errors	7	92	1	11	89	0
Giving stars or other credits for good work	5	90	5	4	87	9
Expecting children to seek permission before leaving the classroom	6	94	0	10	88	2
Punishing children for persistent disruptive behaviour	7	89	4	8	84	7
Teaching children to write clearly	9	91	0	11	88	1
Teaching children to know their multiplication tables by heart	8	92	0	5	93	2

7.8 Progressive methods

	Controlled			Aided		
	M%	S%	L%	M%	S%	L%
Adopting an integrated day	4	92	4	0	96	4
Encouraging self expression	9	90	0	20	79	1
Following a project approach to learning	4	92	3	4	93	3
Generally allowing children to talk to one another	2	96	2	6	91	4
Generally allowing children to decide where they sit	3	92	5	4	87	9
Generally allowing children to move around the classroom	2	94	4	3	91	6

Partnership in Rural Education

8.1 Scale of attitude towards the church school system

Scale item	Corrected item-total correlation
I applied for my present post specifically because it was in a Church of England school	+.5069
The Church of England has too many schools	-.5400
There is no such thing as a specifically Christian view of education	-.3833
The Church of England should develop more secondary/middle/upper schools	+.5819
Church of England schools should teach their pupils about the communion service	+.5184
The Church of England school system has outlived its usefulness	-.6212
Christian education is the job of parents and the church, not schools	-.4033
It is not the task of Church of England schools to initiate children into a religious faith	-.2915
Church of England schools should be given over to the state	-.6069
Church of England schools should encourage pupils to accept the Christian faith	+.4939
The diocese should foster links between Church of England schools and local churches	+.5239
It is educationally unsound for Church of England schools to try to teach the Christian faith	-.4453
Church of England schools are racially divisive	-.3448
The idea of 'worshipping' God in school assembly should be abandoned	-.4376
Anglican parents should be encouraged to send their children to a Church of England school	+.5434
The Church of England spends too much money on church schools	-.4591

8.2 Scale of attitude towards the distinctiveness of church schools

Scale item	Corrected item-total correlation
Teaching about Jesus	+.8282
Putting into practise Christian values	+.6448
Having RE taught by a committed Christian	+.6652
Providing an atmosphere of Christian community	+.7390
Saying classroom prayers	+.6426
Developing close contacts with clergy	+.6699
Integrating religious and secular studies	+.5333
Teaching about God	+.8065
Teaching about Christianity	+.8115
Encouraging regular visits from clergy	+.6704
Providing a daily Christian assembly	+.7373
Teaching about the bible	+.7490
Providing a regular Christian assembly	+.8322
Having committed Christians on the staff	+.6866
Teaching RE	+.7133
Teaching about the church	+.6040

8.3 Scale of attitude towards traditional teaching methods

Scale item	Corrected item-total correlation
Promoting a high level of academic attainment	+.4433
Giving stars or credits for good work	+.3953
Punishing children for persistent disruptive behaviour	+.5208
Training children in hard work	+.5517
Giving regular maths tests	+.6119
Bringing the best out of bright pupils	+.5201
Teaching children to read	+.4817
Teaching children to know their multiplication tables by heart	+.6579
Teaching children to be tidy	+.5936
Teaching children to write clearly	+.5473
Following a regular timetable for different lessons	+.4599
Adopting strict discipline	+.4943
Correcting most spelling and grammatical errors	+.6059
Giving regular spelling tests	+.6461
Expecting children to seek permission before leaving the classroom	+.5573
Adopting firm discipline	+.5777

BIBLIOGRAPHY

Aspin, D.N. (1983) Church schools, religious education and the multi-ethnic community, *Journal of Philosophy of Education*, 17, 229-240.

Boyle, J.J. and Francis, L.J. (in press) The influence of differing church aided school systems on pupil attitude towards religion, *Research in Education*.

Brooksbank, K., Revell, J., Ackstine, E. and Bailey, K. (1982) *County and Voluntary Schools*, Harlow, Councils and Education Press.

Burgess, H.J. (1958) *Enterprise in Education*, London, NS and SPCK.

Camberwell Papers (1979) *The Church in Education: a resource for discussion*, London, Church House.

Cambridge Policy Study in Education (1981) *A Positive Approach to Rural Primary Schools*, Cambridge, Institute of Education.

Carlisle Commission (1971) *Partners in Education: the role of the diocese*, London, NS and SPCK.

Catholic Education in a Multiracial, Multicultural Society (1984) *Learning from Diversity: a challenge for catholic education*, London, Catholic Media Office.

Comber, L.C., Joyce, F.E., Meyenn, R.J., Sinclaire, C.W., Small, M.A., Tricker, M.J. and Whitfield, R.C. (1981) *The Social Effects of Rural Primary School Reorganisation in England*, Birmingham, University of Aston.

Cruickshank, M. (1963) *Church and State in English Education*, London, Macmillan.

Cruickshank, M. (1972) The denominational school issue in the twentieth century, *History in Education*, 1, 200-213.

Dent, H.C. (1947) *The Education Act, 1944: provisions, possibilities and some problems*, London, University of London Press.

Department of Education and Science (1985) *Better Schools*, London, HMSO.

Design Study (1975) *Small Rural Primary Schools in Wales*, Cardiff, The Welsh Office.

Durham Report (1970) *The Fourth R: the report of the commission on religious education in schools*, London, NS and SPCK.

Fahy, P.S. (1980) The religious effectiveness of some Australian catholic high schools, *Word in Life*, 28, 86-98.

Flynn, M.F. (1975) *Some Catholic Schools in Action*, Sydney, Catholic Education Office.

Forsythe, D., *et al.* (1983) *The Rural Community and the Small School*, Aberdeen, Aberdeen University Press.

Francis, L.J. (1979) School influence and pupil attitude towards religion, *British Journal of Educational Psychology*, 49, 107-123.

Francis, L.J. (1983) The logic of education, theology and the church school, *Oxford Review of Education*, 9, 147-162.

Francis, L.J. (1983) Anglican voluntary primary schools and child church attendance, *Research in Education*, 30, 1-9.

Francis, L.J. (1984) *Assessing the Partnership, 1944-1984*, Abingdon, Culham College Institute, Occasional Paper Number 5.

Francis, L.J. (1985) *Rural Anglicanism: a future for young Christians?*, London, Collins Liturgical Publications.

Francis, L.J. and Carter, M. (1980) Church aided secondary schools, religious education as an examination subject and pupil attitude towards religion, *British Journal of Educational Psychology*, 50, 297-300.

Free Church Federal Council Education Committee (1984) *Church Schools*, London, Free Church Federal Council.

Gay, J.D., *et al.* (1982) *The Debate about Church Schools in the Oxford Diocese*, Abingdon, Culham College Institute.

Gay, J.D. (1985) *Between Church and Chalkface*, Abingdon, Culham College Institute, Occasional Paper Number 6.

Gay, J.D. (1985) *The Size of Anglican Primary Schools*, Abingdon, Culham College Institute, Occasional Paper Number 7.

General Synod of the Church of England Board of Education (1984) *Schools and Multi-cultural Education*, London, Church House.

Gittins Report (1967) *Primary Education in Wales*, Cardiff, HMSO.

Greeley, A.M., McCready, W.C. and McCourt, K. (1976) *Catholic Schools in a Declining Church*, Kansas City, Sheed & Ward.

Greeley, A.M. and Rossi, P.H. (1966) *The Education of Catholic Americans*, Chicago, Aldine.

Green, R.H. (1982) *Church Schools: a matter of opinion*, London, Southwark Diocesan Board of Education.

Green, R.H. (1985) *Continuing the Church Schools Debate*, Salisbury, Salisbury Diocesan Education Centre.

Hirst, P.H. (1981) Education, catechesis and the church school, *British Journal of Religious Education*, 3, 85-93.

Hornsby-Smith, M.P. (1978) *Catholic Education: the unobtrusive partner*, London, Sheed & Ward.

Hough, J.R. (1981) *A Study of School Costs*, Windsor, NFER - Nelson.

Howells, R.A. (1982) *Curriculum Provision in the Small Primary School*, Cambridge, Institute of Education.

Joyce, F. and Whitfield, R. (1979) *The Social Effects of Rural Primary School Re-organisation: a study on behalf of the DOE and DES, first interim report*, Birmingham, University of Aston.

Kelly, S.E. (1978) The schools of the established church in England: a study of diocesan involvement since 1944, unpublished Ph.D. dissertation, University of Keele.

Louden, L. (1983) The managers of Blackburn diocese and the implementation of the 1944 Education Act in Lancashire, *Journal of Educational Administration and History*, 15, 1, 10-21.

Louden, L. and Urwin, D.S. (1984) Aided school governors: their role and training, *School Organisation*, 4, 245-264.

Murphy, J. (1971) *Church, State and Schools in Britain: 1800-1970*, London, Routledge & Kegan Paul.

Nash, R. (1980) *Schooling in Rural Societies*, London, Methuen.

National Society (1984) *A Future in Partnership*, London, Church House.

Neuwein, R.A. (Ed.) (1960) *Catholic Schools in Action*, Notre Dame, Indiana, University of Notre Dame Press.

Partners in Mission Consultation (1981) *To a Rebellious House?*, London, CIO Publishing.

Plowden Report (1967) *Children and their Primary Schools*, London, HMSO.

Rhymer, J. and Francis, L.J. (1985) Roman Catholic secondary schools in Scotland and pupil attitude towards religion, *Lumen Vitae*, 40, 103-110.

Rogers, R. (1977) Closing the village schools: what the LEAs are up to, *Where*, 133, 276-280.

Rogers, R. (1979) *Schools under Threat: a handbook on closure*, London, Advisory Centre for Education.

Swann Report (1985) *Education for All*, London, HMSO.

Tirrell, C.B. (1976) *The Aided Schools Handbook*, London, NS and SPCK.

Watkins, R., Derrick, D., *et al.* (1980) *Educational Disadvantage in Rural Areas*, Manchester, Centre for Information and Advice on Educational Disadvantage.

Wiltshire County Council Education Committee (1969) *Small Rural Schools in Wiltshire*, Trowbridge, County Hall.

MAPS

The two maps in this section contrast the provision of church schools within the diocese of St Edmundsbury and Ipswich in 1915 and 1984. The numerical reference before each place name gives the map number or numbers and the letter code gives the grid square in which the place appears. For example, Ipswich is identified as appearing in the grid square Fb; the fact that Ipswich appears on both map 1 and map 2 is indicated by the reference 1, 2.

1, 2	Cb	Acton	1	Hc	Campsea Ash	1	De	Fakenham
1	Ic	Aldeburgh	1, 2	Ea	Capel St Mary	1	Dc	Felsham
1	Hb	Alderton	1, 2	Cb	Cavendish	1, 2	Ed	Finningham
1	Cc	Alpheton	1	Bd	Cavenham	1	Cd	Flempton
1	Ce	Ampton	1, 2	Gc	Charsfield	1, 2	Hf	Flixton
1	Gd	Ashfield	1, 2	Bc	Chedburgh	1	Cd	Fornham St Martin
1	Fd	Aspall	1, 2	Ga	Chelmondiston	1, 2	Gd	Framlingham
1	Hd	Badingham	1	Db	Chelsworth	1	Ae	Freckenham
1, 2	Dd	Badwell Ash	1, 2	Bc	Chevington	1, 2	Ge	Fressingfield
1, 2	De	Bardwell	1	Hc	Chillesford	1	Fa	Freston
1	Fc	Barham	1, 2	Dc	Cockfield	1	If	Frostenden
1, 2	Ce	Barnham	1	Fc	Coddenham	1, 2	Bd	Gazeley
1, 2	De	Barningham	1	De	Coney Weston	1, 2	Ee	Gislingham
1, 2	Bd	Barrow	1, 2	He	Cookley	1, 2	Cd	Great Barton
1	Hf	Barsham	1	Ed	Cotton	1	Ac	Great Bradley
1, 2	Hb	Bawdsey	1	Hd	Cransford	1	Ec	Great Bricett
1	Fc	Baylham	1	He	Cratfield	1, 2	Ec	Great Finborough
1	Ig	Beccles	1, 2	Ec	Creeting St Mary	1	Hd	Great Glemham
1, 2	Gd	Bedfield	1	Fc	Crowfield	1	Ce	Great Livermere
1, 2	Fd	Bedingfield	1, 2	Ce	Culford	1	Bd	Great Saxham
1, 2	Hd	Benhall	1	Bd	Dalham	1	Ac	Great Thurlow
1, 2	Fa	Bentley	1	Gc	Dallinghoo	1, 2	Db	Great Waldingfield
1	Hc	Blaxhall	1	Gc	Debach	1, 2	Cc	Great Whelnetham
1, 2	Db	Boxford	1, 2	Fd	Debenham	1	Db	Groton
1, 2	Hb	Boyton	1	Bd	Denham (Bury	1	Hc	Hacheston
1	Cc	Bradfield Combust			St Edmunds)	1, 2	Eb	Hadleigh
1	Dc	Bradfield St Clare	1	Fe	Denham (Eye)	1	He	Halesworth
1, 2	Dc	Bradfield St George	1, 2	Gd	Dennington	1	Bd	Hargrave
1	Fe	Braiseworth	1	Bc	Denston	1	Fa	Harkstead
1, 2	Ie	Bramfield	1, 2	Dd	Drinkstone	1, 2	Cc	Hartest
1, 2	Fb	Bramford	1	Ie	Dunwich	1	Gc	Hasketon
1, 2	If	Brampton	1	Fc	Earl Stonham	1, 2	Ed	Haughley
1	Fa	Brantham	1, 2	Ea	East Bergholt	1	Bc	Hawkedon
1	Db	Brent Eleigh	1	Gc	Easton	1	Cc	Hawstead
1	Dc	Brettenham	1	Db	Edwardstone	1	Fc	Helmingham
1	Fe	Brome	1, 2	Eb	Elmsett	1	If	Henstead
1	Hc	Bromeswell	1	Dd	Elmswell	1, 2	De	Hepworth
1, 2	Da	Bures	1, 2	Cf	Elveden	1	Bd	Herringswell
1	Ee	Burgate	1	Be	Eriswell	1	Dd	Hessett
1	Eb	Burstall	1	Ce	Euston	1	He	Heveningham
1, 2	Cd	Bury St Edmunds	1, 2	Fe	Eye	1	Ea	Higham
1, 2	Hc	Butley	1, 2	Hc	Eyke	1	Ee	Hinderclay

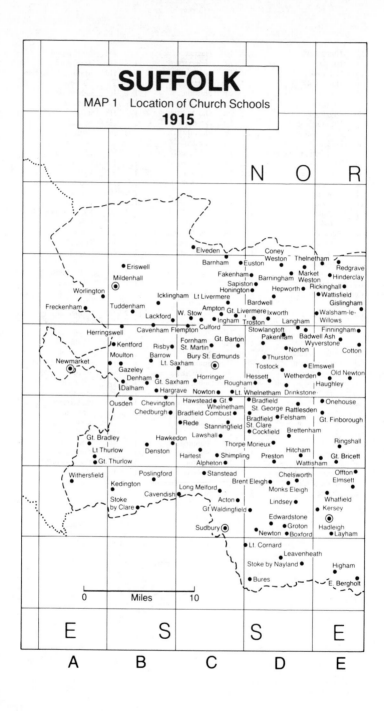

SUFFOLK

MAP 1 Location of Church Schools
1915

N O R

Elveden
Coney
Weston Thelnetham
Barnham Euston
Eriswell Fakenham Market Redgrave
Mildenhall Barningham Weston Hinderclay
Sapiston Rickinghall
Worlington Honington Hepworth Wattisfield
Icklingham Lt Livermere Gislingham
Freckenham Tuddenham Bardwell
Ampton Gt Livermere Ixworth Walsham-le-
Lackford W. Stow Ingham Troston Langham Willows
Cavenham Flempton Culford
Herringswell Stowlangtoft Finningham
Kentford Fornham Gt. Barton Pakenham Badwell Ash
Risby St. Martin Wyverstone
Moulton Barrow Bury St. Edmunds Norton Cotton
Newmarket Lt. Saxham Thurston
Gazeley Tostock Elmswell Old Newton
Denham Horringer Hessett Wetherden
Dalham Gt. Saxham Rougham Haughley
Hargrave Nowton Lt. Whelnetham Drinkstone
Hawstead Gt. Bradfield Onehouse
Ousden Chevington Whelnetham St. George Rattlesden
Chedburgh Bradfield Combust Bradfield Felsham Gt. Finborough
Rede St. Clare
Gt. Bradley Hawkedon Lawshall Stanningfield Brettenham Ringshall
Lt Thurlow Denston Thorpe Morieux
Gt. Thurlow Hartest Shimpling Hitcham Gt. Bricett
Withersfield Alpheton Preston Wattisham
Stanstead Chelsworth Offton
Poslingford Brent Eleigh Elmsett
Kedington Long Melford Monks Eleigh
Cavendish Acton Lindsey Whatfield
Stoke Gt Waldingfield Kersey
by Clare Edwardstone
Sudbury Groton Hadleigh
Newton Boxford Layham
Lt. Cornard
Leavenheath
Stoke by Nayland Higham
Bures E. Bergholt

0 Miles 10

E S S E

A B C D E

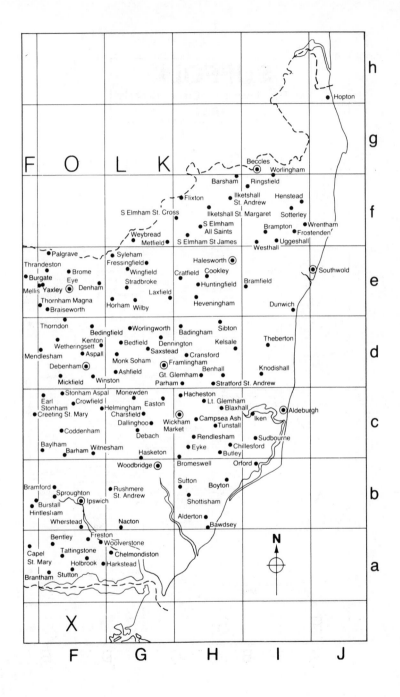

h

g

F O L K

Hopton

Beccles
Worlingham

Barsham Ringsfield

Flixton Ilketshall Henstead
St. Andrew

S Elmham St. Cross Ilketshall St. Margaret Sotterley

f

S Elmham Brampton Wrentham
All Saints Frostenden

Weybread S Elmham St James Uggeshall
Metfield Westhall

Palgrave Syleham
Thrandeston Fressingfield Halesworth Southwold
Brome Wingfield Cratfield Cookley
Burgate Eye Bramfield
Mellis Yaxley Denham Stradbroke
Huntingfield
Laxfield
Thornham Magna Heveningham Dunwich
Braiseworth Horham Wilby

e

Thorndon Worlingworth Badingham Sibton
Bedingfield Theberton
Kenton Bedfield Dennington Kelsale
Wetheringsett Saxstead Cransford
Mendlesham Aspall Framlingham Knodishall
Debenham Monk Soham Benhall
Mickfield Ashfield Gt. Glemham
Winston Parham Stratford St. Andrew

d

Stonham Aspal Monewden Hacheston
Earl Crowfield Easton Lt. Glemham
Stonham Helmingham Blaxhall Aldeburgh
Creeting St. Mary Charsfield Campsea Ash Iken
Dallinghoo Wickham Tunstall
Coddenham Market
Debach Rendlesham Sudbourne
Baylham Eyke Chillesford
Barham Witnesham Butley
Hasketon

c

Woodbridge Bromeswell Orford

Sutton
Bramford Boyton
Sproughton Rushmere
St. Andrew Shottisham
Burstall Ipswich
Hintlesham Alderton
Wherstead Nacton Bawdsey

b

Bentley Freston
Tattingstone Woolverstone N
Capel Chelmondiston
St. Mary Holbrook Harkstead
Brantham Stutton

a

X

F   G   H   I   J

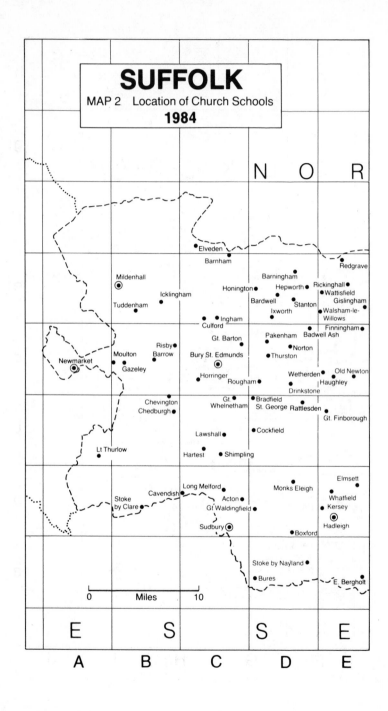

SUFFOLK

MAP 2 Location of Church Schools
1984

N O R

Elveden

Barnham

Redgrave

Mildenhall

Barningham

Honington   Hepworth   Rickinghall
                                          Wattisfield
Bardwell   Stanton   Gislingham
            Ixworth   Walsham-le-
                                          Willows

Icklingham

Tuddenham

Ingham

Culford   Finningham

Gt. Barton   Pakenham   Badwell Ash

Risby
Barrow   Norton
Moulton   Bury St. Edmunds   Thurston
Newmarket   Gazeley
                                    Wetherden   Old Newton
                        Horringer   Haughley
                            Rougham
                                        Drinkstone

Chevington   Gt.   Bradfield
Chedburgh   Whelnetham St. George Rattlesden
                                                Gt. Finborough

                    Lawshall   Cockfield

Lt Thurlow   Hartest   Shimpling

                                                    Elmsett
            Long Melford   Monks Eleigh
Cavendish   Whatfield
Stoke   Acton   Kersey
by Clare   Gt Waldingfield
                                                  Hadleigh
            Sudbury
                                Boxford

                    Stoke by Nayland
                        Bures   E. Bergholt

0   Miles   10

E   S   S   E

A   B   C   D   E

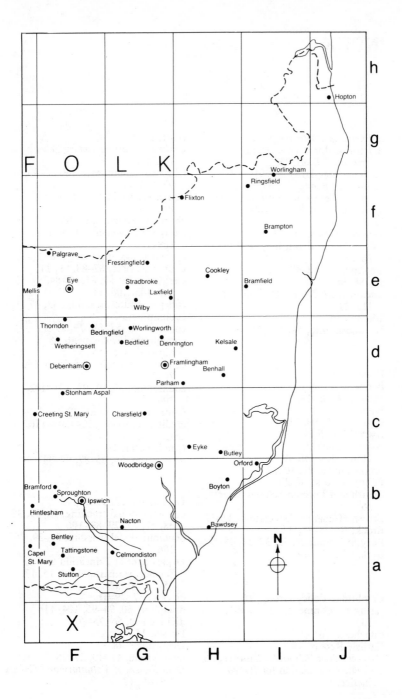

h

Hopton

g

F O L K
Worlingham

Ringsfield

Flixton

f

Brampton

Palgrave
Fressingfield
Cookley
Eye
Stradbroke
Bramfield

e

Mellis
Laxfield
Wilby

Thorndon
Bedingfield
Worlingworth
Wetheringsett
Bedfield
Dennington
Kelsale

d

Debenham
Framlingham
Benhall
Parham

Stonham Aspal

Creeting St. Mary
Charsfield

c

Eyke
Butley
Woodbridge
Orford

Bramford
Boyton

b

Sproughton
Ipswich
Hintlesham

Nacton
Bawdsey

Bentley
N

Capel
St. Mary
Tattingstone
Celmondiston

a

Stutton

X

F   G   H   I   J

INDEX